The Priestess and the Pen is an important and radical first revelation of how mythic fiction has affected modern Paganism...*The Priestess and the Pen* points a way forward based on concepts from the past, our inner genetic motivations, and a strong view that we all—as represented by the priestess of Pagan practice—can be more than we are.

DONALD MICHAEL KRAIG

THE PRIESTESS & THE *Pen*

About the Author

Sonja Sadovsky (Tampa, Florida) holds a degree in creative writing from the University of South Florida and an MA in religious studies with a concentration in Western esotericism and mysticism from the University of Amsterdam, the Netherlands. She lectures on Wicca, Kabbalah, and Western esotericism in the modern context.

THE PRIESTESS & THE *Pen*

Marion Zimmer Bradley, Dion Fortune, and
Diana Paxson's Influence on Modern Paganism

SONJA SADOVSKY

Llewellyn Publications
Woodbury, Minnesota

The Priestess and the Pen: Marion Zimmer Bradley, Dion Fortune, and Diana Paxson's Influence on Modern Paganism © 2014 by Sonja Sadovsky. All rights reserved. No part of this book may be used or reproduced in any manner whatsoever, including Internet usage, without written permission from Llewellyn Publications, except in the case of brief quotations embodied in critical articles and reviews.

FIRST EDITION
First Printing, 2014

Book design by Rebecca Zins
Cover design by Ellen Lawson
Cover art: Art Resource, Inc., image #ART137678, *The Magic Circle*, John William Waterhouse; photo credit: Tate, London/Art Resource, NY
Photo of H. P. Blavatsky courtesy of Theosophical Society in America Archives
Photo of Marion Zimmer Bradley © Modern Arts Studio, Oakland, CA
Photo of Dion Fortune © 2013 The Society of the Inner Light
Photo of Diana Paxson © 2014 Mike Stalnaker

Llewellyn is a registered trademark of Llewellyn Worldwide Ltd.

Library of Congress Cataloging-in-Publication Data
Sadovsky, Sonja, 1980–
  The priestess and the pen : Marion Zimmer Bradley, Dion Fortune, and Diana Paxson's influence on modern paganism / Sonja Sadovsky.—First edition.
      pages cm
  Includes bibliographical references and index.
  ISBN 978-0-7387-3800-0
  1. Fantasy fiction, American—History and criticism. 2. Fantasy fiction, English—History and criticism. 3. Heroines in literature. 4. Occultism in literature. 5. Paganism in literature. 6. Women priests in literature. 7. Bradley, Marion Zimmer—Influence. 8. Fortune, Dion—Influence. 9. Paxson, Diana L.—Influence. I. Title.
  PS374.F27S33 2014
  813'.0876609—dc23
                                                                    2014028498

Llewellyn Worldwide does not participate in, endorse, or have any authority or responsibility concerning private business transactions between our authors and the public.

All mail addressed to the author is forwarded, but the publisher cannot, unless specifically instructed by the author, give out an address or phone number.

Any Internet references contained in this work are current at publication time, but the publisher cannot guarantee that a specific location will continue to be maintained. Please refer to the publisher's website for links to authors' websites and other sources.

Llewellyn Publications
A Division of Llewellyn Worldwide Ltd.
2143 Woodcdale Drive
Woodbury, MN 55125-2989

www.llewellyn.com

Printed in the United States of America

For Don and everyone else
who dares to live the dream.

CONTENTS

Foreword by Donald Michael Kraig xi

Preface xxi

Introduction 1

CHAPTER 1: Women, Literature, and the Occult in the Modern Era ... 11

CHAPTER 2: Dion Fortune / Violet Firth ... 31

CHAPTER 3: Earth Mother / Moon Mistress ... 41

CHAPTER 4: Marion Zimmer Bradley ... 57

CHAPTER 5: Witch Queen ... 69

CHAPTER 6: Diana L. Paxson ... 85

Chapter 7: Warrior Queen ... 105

Chapter 8: The Priestess and the Problem of Feminine Evil ... 123

Chapter 9: New Frontiers ... 153

Appendix ... 177

Exercise: Automatic Writing ... 189

Acknowledgments   *193*

Bibliography   *195*

Index   *199*

FOREWORD

Although news articles, comments by political pundits, and advertisements from for-profit colleges continually focus on how much money you can make after you graduate from college, traditional universities prefer to help young students broaden their interests and become generally knowledgeable in a wide area of scientific, philosophical, and cultural areas, becoming more well-rounded as individuals and citizens. A student's major—their area of focus—often doesn't become apparent until the student has spent two years in college.

Besides those general courses and the core courses of their majors, students have a variety of courses from which to choose that expand upon the core of their major. These classes, as well as general classes needed to fulfill graduation requirements, are called electives. So students can focus on their core classes, they often try to take electives that have little work and make it easy to earn an A grade. When I attended UCLA, these classes were collectively known as "Mickey Mouse" courses, although they're also known as "gut, pipe, slide, fluff" or even "loan-saver" classes. There are many more terms for such courses, too.

And like other students, there came a time when I needed such a course. One that fit my schedule during my junior year was Children's Literature—"kiddie lit"—and it had a reputation for being just what I needed. Unexpectedly, it turned out to be quite challenging and had well over a thousand pages of required reading.

Still, the class itself was fun. One day, the professor came in a few minutes late. He placed the briefcase he was carrying on the podium, opened it, and pulled out a jump rope. To our amazement, he proceeded to use the jump rope (including several fancy tricks) while reciting a jumping rhyme. When he finished—and while he caught his breath—we all applauded. He asked if anyone had heard that rhyme before. Most of the three hundred or so people in the class raised their hands. Then he asked if anyone had used a different version of the rhyme. Most of the rest of the lesson consisted of students describing the different versions they had used in their younger days.

In the last minutes of the class the professor explained how rhymes, like children's stories, change due to local history, customs, and traditions. Often, however, there were similarities, and it was that underlying similarity that was important.

In a following class, our professor discussed the works of a lecturer known for his studies in comparative mythology, Joseph Campbell. Campbell is perhaps best known for his book and TV series *The Power of Myth*. However, in what is arguably his most important work, *The Hero with a Thousand Faces*, Campbell introduced the idea that there is an important and universal myth found in countless books, stories, and legends. George Lucas eventually used this concept when he wrote *Star Wars*, and perhaps that's why the film has become so culturally significant. Campbell called the concept of this archetypal myth "the hero's journey."

According to Campbell, the journey has twelve aspects: (1) The hero is somewhat of an outcast or outsider in his everyday world. (2) He's called to go on an adventure, but he (3) refuses the call. (4) He meets a mentor who trains him, and (5) he leaves his ordinary world behind. (6) He meets all sorts of tests and develops allies, but (7) moves toward something momentous. (8) He faces his death and/or his greatest fear, and (9) he comes out with new wisdom or some sort of skill or treasure. (10) Now he has to return to his original home with his treasure, where (11) he is tested once more, perhaps going through death to rebirth, victorious at last. (12) He either stays there with his treasure or moves on to new journeys, transformed by the experience.

At the time, I was also spending lots of hours at Melnitz Hall studying motion picture/television production and direction, which I hoped to make my major. To understand the challenges of actors, I took an acting class that was being taught by a playwright. He introduced us to the ideas of the creator of method acting, Constantin Stanislavsky. Part of the method was to find what is good, positive, and human in the most evil characters and bring that out in your acting. Similarly, actors should bring out the failures, flaws, and negativity within heroes. In this way the characters become more real. A good playwright will either allude to such characteristics or directly include them. If they're not there, the actor using the method creates them by inventing an appropriate backstory, perhaps from the character's birth to the appearance in the movie or play.

While I found that fascinating on a practical level, what really interested me was the professor's introduction to some of Carl Jung's ideas. Specifically, he introduced us to Jung's idea that we have within us an opposite aspect, a shadow, and we must come to terms with it in order to achieve wholeness, or "individuation." Jung characterized this in terms of masculine (animus) and feminine (anima), and added that we have both positive and negative aspects to our shadow, a good mother and an evil mother. The evil mother is often represented by an old woman or "witch" or by a universal evil mother/feminine image such as a dark cave. We each need to enter the cave or deal with the evil mother and integrate her into ourselves.

To me, this was the part that had been left out of the discussion of Campbell's journey. The journey is essentially an externalization of interior development. It's not really about the hero doing things out there, it's about us becoming healthy and mature adults. We're attracted to stories that follow the hero's journey because they are, in essence, about our own struggles to achieve self-empowerment and wholeness.

And that brings me back to kiddie lit. In addition to the voluminous amount of required reading, one of the additional books we had a choice of reading was *A Wizard of Earthsea* by Ursula K. Le Guin. As I read it, I literally saw the entirety of Campbell, Stanislavsky, and Jung being played out before me on an epic scale, and I became enthralled with these concepts.

By the time I graduated from college, I had also been involved with the study of magick and occultism for several years. One of the things I noticed was that certain aspects of the fictional writings of Dion Fortune and Aleister Crowley were absolutely breathtaking. I specifically liked Fortune's *The Sea Priestess* and *Moon Magic* as well as Crowley's *Moonchild*, his terrifying *Diary of a Drug Fiend*, and his surrealistic dream *The Wake World*. And while striking and often including mystical symbolism, to me they were just fiction; that was all.

About two years later I was living in Encinitas, California, and after studying and practicing on my own, as well as being a member of several magickal and spiritual groups, I was beginning to teach classes on occult topics. I happened to read that Le Guin was giving a book signing nearby. I took my well-worn copy of *Earthsea* with me and went to see her.

She gave a brief reading from her latest book and then started signing copies. I patiently waited in line. Everyone had purchased new books for her to sign…everyone except me. I told her I was sorry and that I only had this old and much-loved copy that I'd like her to sign.

To my surprise, she started thumbing through it, and her face seemed to light up and sparkle. She said, "I'm delighted to see that someone is actually reading this." I asked her if she was going to write any more in the Earthsea series of books (at that time, there were only three that had been published). Her answer surprised and changed me. "I don't know," she said. "Ged (the main character) doesn't speak to me anymore."

I walked away stunned. I knew that some nonfiction spiritual books were inspired or channeled. I also knew that the same was true of some fiction books. Quite frankly, though, I had found most so-called channeled or inspired works to be of questionable value, perhaps due to their frequently horrendous writing styles. But if the beautiful and mythic artistry of Le Guin were the result of her "talking" with Ged, what of some of the other great fictions that can influence us deeply?

On any Halloween night in any street in America, you can see young girls who dress up as princesses or Disney-influenced Snow Whites. If the dreams of such wishes have inculcated themselves in these girls' psyches, how will that influence their approach to occultism if they grow up to be real witches and magicians? Young boys dress up to be Luke Skywalker or a Teenage Mutant Ninja Turtle. They fight imagined evil for what seems like lost causes. How will this attitude seep into their psyches and influence the way they think and act in the future?

While sociological studies and wild assumptions abound—ranging from the fantasy that comic books cause juvenile delinquency promulgated by Fredric Wertham's 1954 *Seduction of the Innocents* (resulting in fifty years of self-censorship by the Comics Code Authority) to the current socio-political meme being promoted by gun manufacturers and their defenders that video games (which sell in the tens of millions) cause gun deaths—little that I know of, until now, has looked at the effects of spiritually induced fiction on modern occultism.

Llewellyn Worldwide, the publisher of this book, has always published books for all ranges of students, readers, and practitioners. Since in any field of study there are always more beginners than advanced students, it was obvious that Llewellyn would publish more books for beginners. That, however, does not justify the belief among some people that Llewellyn only publishes books for beginners, a few even saying that we only published books intended for "fluffy bunnies." Llewellyn has published and continues to publish intermediate and advanced books in all areas of spirituality, including astrology, Paganism, Wicca, and ceremonial magick.

When I was asked to add to my work with Llewellyn by becoming an acquisitions editor, I was thrilled with my assignment to especially find books that were more advanced. I just had one major challenge: where would I find authors writing these kinds of books?

Shortly after obtaining my additional assignment, I went on tour to lecture at several Pagan events across the country. I met Sonja Sadovsky in Florida and we immediately hit it off, becoming friends. She shared some of the ideas she had written for her university master's thesis. I asked to see it, and she sent me a copy. I knew this needed to be my first acquisition of more advanced books.

The Priestess and the Pen is an important and radical first revelation of how mythic fiction has affected modern Paganism. When I first started studying and practicing Wicca, it was believed by most of us that Wicca was an ancient religion with some modern additions. By the time Ronald Hutton published *The Triumph of the Moon* in 1999, most Pagans, or at least most of the leaders and writers on Wicca and witchcraft, acknowledged that objective historical records did not support this claim. Wicca was based on ancient concepts and beliefs combined with modern ones, but it was not itself ancient.

Wicca could and needed to stand on its own without relying on a false history. Hutton and his followers refer to his newer and more historically accurate understanding as a revisionist interpretation of the history of Wicca, as it revises the original "Wicca is ancient" belief. This critical self-analysis occurred only fifty years after Wicca started to become known. It is arguable that the same didn't happen with Christianity until the Enlightenment, more then 1,500 years after its birth.

It is impossible to separate the myths and beliefs of childhood that we now simply accept not as facts, but as "the way things are"—truisms that control our so-called logical interpretations of reality. We cry out that we have free will, yet we are literally controlled by those ideas and concepts that have become embedded in our unconscious minds. They form a lens through which we filter the light of the physical universe.

Some of these metaphorical lenses we peer through were not established within us from our youth. Instead, they come from those myths that are hardwired into us—the hero's journey and the Jungian goal of individuation as well as the drive to self-actualization as described by Kurt Goldstein, Carl Rogers, and Abraham Maslow. It is likely that these concepts have informed trance-induced or unconsciously inspired fiction and that those fictions have played powerful roles in the creation of the images and practices we accept and believe, and which have become manifest in the nonfiction writings of Pagan leaders. *The Priestess and the Pen* moves us from the mere historical reality of Hutton's revisionist filter to an understanding of the psycho-spiritual impact of past fiction on Paganism today. A new aeon of Paganism has begun

I believe that this book will open a door that goes beyond the superficiality of an accurate objective history of modern Paganism, no matter how necessary that may have been. It will begin to show the spiritual and psychological core that has made modern Paganism one of the fastest-growing spiritual paths in the world. Without this core, Paganism would be nothing more than a fad like hula hoops and the Macarena.

Rather than taking on all of Paganism, Sadovsky wisely chooses just to look at one element: the priestess and her nature. Its surprising conclusion—that the priestess (and, therefore, the Goddess whom the priestess represents) has four faces and not just three—may take some time to become better known and accepted, but the strength and self-empowerment it represents for women and men could be as important as the modern acceptance of the Goddess herself.

Religions and spiritual traditions either evolve to meet the needs of the people over time or become corrosive and dogmatic, resulting in religious leaders sometimes needing to support violent repression of any alternatives; we can see that now among some fundamentalist religious sects. *The Priestess and the Pen* points a way forward based on concepts from the past, our inner genetic motivations, and a strong view that we all—as represented by the priestess of Pagan practice—can be more than we are.

As a result, this book is far more than simply an accurate historical record, an instruction manual, or yet another set of spells with questionable antiquity or effectiveness. It points to the psychological background dwelling in each of our unconscious minds that manifested through certain fiction and influenced our formulators and leaders, and that over the past half-century-plus has resulted in the vibrant and exciting outburst of spirituality known as Paganism, Wicca, and modern Witchcraft.

I sometimes wonder if the early modern expositors of Wicca and Paganism understood the psychological needs and underpinnings of what they presented or how it would change the world. I wonder if they were aware of their own inner motivations and drives that colored their books, lectures, and very presence. *The Priestess and the Pen* finally reveals, through example, these inner secrets, which will allow Wicca and Witchcraft to grow and evolve even more, allowing future generations to find guidance and succor for their lives.

Donald Michael Kraig

PREFACE

I LOVE TO read and have always been a bookworm. I devour stories like a book blight, reading several at once. Books have always been my solace against conflict. There is nothing more soothing to my nerves than the weight of a new or favorite book in hand. There is something about the tactile pleasure of thumbing through the pages, inhaling the scent of the paper, and settling into a good read that thrills me. At times, this passion for books absorbs me completely, and I am gone for days, caught up in the adventure until the journey is over. Although I am omnivorous when it comes to reading, there are certain themes that have come to dominate my library over the years and attest to a long love affair with science fiction, fantasy, alternative philosophies, comparative religion, and magic.

My favorite stories have always featured witches and sorceresses, warrior women and queens. The image of the powerful woman, whether she is a hero or a villain, has fascinated me since I was child. My first taste of these ideas came through fairy tales. Whoever she is—as the Evil Queen casting a curse, the resourceful heroine thwarting the wicked spell, or simply a girl fated for an inexplicable, life-altering event—my favorite female characters all have one thing in common: they use magic to radically alter their life. Magic is the constant variable in each tale. Ever present, it is available to those with the wit and tenacity to access it and use its power for good or for evil. Its consequences are completely dependent upon the character of those who employ it.

Like many kids, I believed in magic. I have always felt that it would work for me if I could just gather the right knowledge to unlock its secrets. Determined to read everything that could help me in this quest, I started collecting tales that featured occult theories, magical realism, mythology, and legends. When I had exhausted all of the relevant children's literature at my local library and bookstore, I started in on adult fiction. I purchased a copy of *The Mists of Avalon* when I was eleven years old and it felt like a gong had gone off in my mind. The book expressed so many of the themes that I had been searching for and introduced me to the concept of the Goddess as well as her earthly counterpart, the priestess.

These ideas resonated so strongly with me that I had no doubt of their authenticity. It made no difference that the story was fiction. The passion and conviction the author put into her images and the complexity of the religion of Avalon convinced me that this writer fully believed in these ideas and that what I was reading was more than just a retelling of an ancient myth. There seemed to be a completely different story hidden between these pages, a secret that was presented in code. I was convinced that divine inspiration had sent the book to me and that this was a clue to something powerful, something real. This was a message to keep searching—that there was far more to be discovered if I possessed the fortitude and patience to glean it.

The image of the priestess burned in my mind and became emblematic of the changes I wished to manifest in my own life. She was magical, educated, empowered, and consecrated to the Goddess for a sacred purpose. I was so excited by these thoughts that I decided to kick my research into high gear, read everything that I could get my hands on that incorporated Goddess themes, and started calling myself a Pagan.

This caused some friction for me, as the adults in my life had gradually begun to realize that my interest in these topics was neither random nor temporary. While my parents were not particularly religious, they were concerned about my growing enthusiasm for occult sciences and alternative philosophies. (There had also been an embarrassing incident when I had attempted to purchase a nonfictional book on Wicca at the local bookstore and was refused service.) My folks were not interested in fueling any deviant behavior that would cause others to think that I was delusional or irrational. I was equally adamant that these subjects were misunderstood and was resolute in my dedication to continue exploring these concepts. It was a stressful time, but eventually we reached a compromise.

As long as I kept my explorations to the hypothetical realm and limited my choices to myths and stories, then I could continue to pick up new books regularly. Nonfictional occult studies or anything deemed objectionable was prohibited and would not be coming home with me. While I was disappointed, I took the deal. Some books were better than no books. Also, I soon realized that this censorship did not impair my research whatsoever. Fiction proved to be a gold mine of the forbidden topics that stimulated my curiosity, and as a bonus they included sexy details and adult dialogue that were absolutely inappropriate for someone my age. I kept quiet, and everyone was happy. This system worked fine for several years and became a sort of ritual in itself.

I would get dropped off at the bookstore, and my mom would run errands or wait outside as I perused the new arrivals. I would head straight to the sci-fi/fantasy section and scope it out. Sometimes sharing a mute greeting with another fan, I would end up meditating on the shelves for at least an hour, combing through them for additions to my favorite series. When pressed for time, my method of selection was simple. Check out the new arrivals for my favorite authors. If no luck there, then grab the one with the best cover art and glance at the back cover for the blurb. Magical women with swords? Dragons or mythical creatures? Priestesses of an arcane sect? Done; proceed to checkout.

Although I enjoy the occasional hard sci-fi futuristic scene with advanced technology, that is not my poison. Aliens threatening mass extinction, killer robots, intergalactic war—these concepts are all entertaining but do not grab me to the point of total immersion. Now toss in some maniacal magicians, pacts with nonhuman entities, revenge killing, and demonic sex, and you've got my attention. Give me blood and magic any day.

As an adult, my interest in these topics translated into college courses of literature and religious studies. There seemed to be a distinct theoretical thread that ran through all of my favorite subjects. Enlightenment philosophy, romantic literature, modern drama—all of these topics and more seemed connected to this web, forming some kind of faint constellation in my mind. I later went overseas to do my graduate work in the Netherlands and completed a master's degree in humanities with a concentration in Western esotericism and mysticism. It was during this time that I was presented with an entirely different perspective on esoteric philosophy and its contributions to Western culture, politics, and history. The tentative connections that I had made as an undergrad were affirmed by the knowledge that there is an alternative to the dominant narrative of history, science, and religion that makes up our contemporary cultural milieu. It became apparent to me that the belief in the supernatural and humankind's ability to interact and manipulate these unseen forces was not merely superstition or aberrant thinking but, in fact, the remnants of a collection of forbidden philosophies that have survived from antiquity and been debated for centuries throughout the world. These theories create an alternative dialogue that continues to have an impact on Western society up to the present day.

Throughout history, this unconventional conversation concerning human potential has been alternately applauded and repressed. It has been construed as irrelevant or extremely dangerous to the construction of a standard narrative. Books have been banned, concepts discredited, and people have perished, all in effort to control access to information in the history of ideas. Some concepts are so radical that they have been deemed by various groups to be too subversive for common consumption; these are routinely edited from the collective conversation through censorship and marginalization. And yet, these same questions and deviant ideas constantly resurface to be debated in secret, if nowhere else.

One such topic that has always appealed to me—and has been debated for generations—is a woman's role in society and her connection to the Divine. I was particularly interested in finding out how the contemporary concept of the Goddess that I had been exposed to fit within the wider framework of Western esotericism.

Determined to investigate these concepts, I began searching through all of the fascinating information and new material available to me. Although there is a significant compendium of esoteric discourse authored by women in the West (the works of Hildegard of Bingen and Anna Kingsford are just two examples), overall there seemed to be a lack of scholarship that significantly investigates and analyzes these concepts from a female perspective. Also, these theories did not lend themselves to immediate identification with the images that were most familiar to me. Instead, my attention returned to the fiction that had first ignited my curiosity in these matters. My interest in the intersection of gender, power, and religion began with those stories of magical women I had read years before; they had retained their potency to capture my attention. This was significant, because by this time I had met other people in my travels who were similarly influenced by the same books that I had read and were engaged in some form of alternative spirituality.

Every woman that I encountered who named herself a Pagan or a priestess had a shelf of "go to" books that she utilized for inspiration and source material. While the nonfictional occult studies in her library varied from place to place, the one constant was the inclusion of a specific genre of fiction and stories written by the three authors who are the focal point of this book. Regardless of the country she resided in, each lady I met had at least one if not several novels by Dion Fortune, Marion Zimmer Bradley, or Diana L. Paxson displayed amongst the important books in her library. This discovery was meaningful because despite the religious diversity and philosophical differences amongst my new acquaintances, every one maintained that these fictional books contained some type of transcendental truth that had inspired them to become the people they had always wanted to be.

I was stunned, as I had read these same stories and experienced a similar reaction. In both a personal and professional sense, I had devoted much of my time, money, and credibility into the pursuit of forbidden knowledge and Goddess-centered spirituality, and I had traveled very far to investigate concepts originally introduced to me as mere fantasy. This led to another surprising revelation. Despite all of the effort and expense I had incurred seeking out obscure esoteric knowledge, it was the books I had started with that would once again become the focal point of my research into the character of the priestess.

The irony of the situation did not escape me; I was both amused and disturbed. It felt like there was some kind of cosmic joke being played out, an invisible raw egg cracking on my head. I had come full circle, re-examining the books of my childhood through a new perspective, and it proved to be an intense experience. Reading these stories through an educated lens led to some vulnerable sensations and deep soul-searching on my part.

It was humbling to realize that this project would not only answer questions that had traveled with me all of these years, but it was also a tacit admission that many of my choices and lifelong pursuits were originally inspired by fiction. It is one thing to think it, another to say it. These thoughts led me to a period of stark self-examination. Why had these books made such an impression upon me at an early age, and why was I so drawn to the images that they portrayed? I started to question whether my identity was truly self-directed or if it was the result of specific stimuli introduced in my formative years. Was the satisfaction that I had found from these ideas and archetypes meaningless? I was afraid to discover through my research that everything I had believed in was nothing more than smoke and mirrors, just an extended exercise in self-deception. Is the Goddess real if I connect with her through fiction?

These thoughts were constantly running through my mind as I embarked upon the first incarnation of this project, which was my master's thesis. It was terrifying and exhilarating attending school overseas. I was immersed in a discipline and analyzing what seemed to be massive amounts of foreign material. We discussed the most controversial subjects and philosophies that I had always wanted to investigate but never had access to. Plus, my choice of topic necessitated me to unpack some personal baggage in order for any of it to make sense. Finally, the project had to be something entirely original, yet documented thoroughly. At times I wondered if I was working up to something great—or working up to a nervous breakdown. It was infuriating and hilarious at the same time.

On the up side, graduate studies forced me to become a much more organized and critical thinker. This helped me sort out the emotions that these questions had caused. I realized that although I had first discovered these ideas through fiction, my personal experience of them was completely real. Regardless of whether these concepts are externally validated, they have had a clear and measurable effect on my own development. The philosophies contained within those stories were the impetus for my unique educational and spiritual choices, resulting in authentic experiences. It became apparent that the source of a theory is less important than the action it inspires. It made no difference whatsoever if I had based my choices on escapist chick lit, the Holy Grail, or a belief in the Great Pumpkin. The important aspect was what I was doing and where I was going with this information, not where my inspiration began.

While I was still young enough to accept this idea, I had also reached the age where long-term implications of this type of thinking are troubling. As a teenager, it is somewhat easier to think you can make it all up as you go along; it is almost a biological imperative. In the back of my mind I had nursed this notion that one day all would be made clear and the events of my life would be merited by something outside of myself. Eventually I would find the *prisca theologia* that would serve as the magic key to unlock the meaning behind the experiences of my life. As an adult I found myself still searching for answers, only to be redirected inward, back to those formative experiences. Now armed with an arsenal of forbidden history and occult knowledge to use as a new lens, it was still up to me to sort through the experiences of my life and glean some sort of meaning from them.

This is the ultimate dilemma of the freethinker. When faced with an existential crisis, do you accept what cannot be proven or do you reject the entire system? I have always endorsed a concept of pantheistic atheism, which translates to either everything is equally valid or all of it is lies; everything is real or nothing is, or maybe both. Personally, I prefer to believe in everything because it is more fun this way. While the ultimate existence of the Goddess may not be empirically provable, the effect she has had on my life is easily demonstrated. I cannot discount myths and legends because of their fictional nature since the concept of the Goddess that they relay has caused a profound and measurable shift in my perception of the world.

Satisfied with this assessment, I was able to move forward with my research. It was apparent that despite the fictional content of these novels, they could be studied within a wider framework of Western esotericism. Each story is a contemporary extension of that ancient conversation debating the relationship between human, nature, and god. The key difference is that these tales are told from a female perspective and include each author's version of an ideal religion or society. The female characters in each novel represent different aspects of the author's concept of female empowerment and her thoughts on a woman's place in society.

The priestess is unique from other female protagonists that appear in the twentieth century because she uses magic to manifest the will of the Goddess and transmits each author's unique occult experience to the audience. I have been extremely fortunate to revisit this concept many years later to complete my analysis and include new material, presenting the expanded version under the title of *The Priestess and the Pen*. The title signifies the process by which each of these authors has contributed to the development of modern Goddess theory in the twentieth century.

The most dynamic representation of this dialogue in contemporary literature is the character of the priestess. She is a symbol of independent female authority and a living link to the Goddess she serves. For more than a century authors have used this motif to explore gender politics, self-identity, and religion. *The Priestess and the Pen* examines the fiction of three women who use the character of the priestess to promote their esoteric ideals. Dion Fortune, in the early twentieth century, was the first author to use this motif to transmit concepts from the Western Mystery Tradition relayed through a female point of view. Marion Zimmer Bradley and Diana L. Paxson, in the later part of the twentieth century to the present day, have adapted the original template created by Fortune to explore their own versions of female empowerment and conceptions of the Goddess through the Avalon series as well as in their solo works. The priestess in contemporary fiction is unique because she represents an ongoing dialogue within Western esotericism about sex and power as told from a female perspective. Far from being limited to these three authors, these concepts continue to be explored by men and women alike. However, I focus on these authors as being pivotal contributors to the contemporary dialogue, who paved the way for our current conversation by concentrating and refining a specific series of related themes in their constructions of the priestess.

The Priestess and the Pen begins by exploring some of the historic connections between women, literature, and occult societies in the modern context, and discusses the role of speculative fiction and the spread of new ideas. Each author is then introduced, and selected works are reviewed for their construction of the priestess and, by extension, the Goddess. If the priestess is the ideal, then who is her evil sister, the sorceress? How does the priestess interact with the world around her, and what is her philosophy? How do nightmares of feminine evil affect the taboos and duties of the priestess? How does the image of the Goddess evolve throughout the twentieth century and change with each author's point of view?

Included is an interview with Diana L. Paxson, who discusses the character of the priestess throughout her works. There is also an exercise in the appendix for those who would like to experiment with automatic or trance writing in order to connect with and identify their own unique vision of the Goddess. The book concludes with some thoughts on the revolutionary nature of the priestess and how this image continues to influence the evolution of the Goddess in the modern era.

INTRODUCTION

IN THIS STUDY we will examine the process by which authors have utilized the fictional character of the priestess to promote female empowerment through the lens of esoteric philosophy. By examining the historical links between occult societies, feminism, and literature, it becomes clear that women have greatly influenced the political and social policies of the modern era. This is a direct result of women participating in alternative religions and philosophies, then debating their ideas in person and in print.

This phenomenon has created a new concept of female identity that is both secular and sacred, as well as a new image of the female divine. In order to achieve this, women in the West adapted the misogynistic images and motifs prevalent in the Victorian Age and inverted ideas of feminine evil and weakness into those of female power and strength. The resultant combination produced the priestess, a woman who uses her sexuality and personal power to heal the wounded psyche and connect people with the Goddess.

This study focuses on the image of the priestess in fiction for the simple reason that fiction is a popular medium that reaches a wider audience than occult nonfiction. She who controls the media controls the message. The women who write about this character in fiction tend to have a larger influence on the meaning of the term because their works are more accessible to the general public.

The authors selected for review in this study all fit the criteria of having participated in alternative religions or occult societies in their private lives before translating their personal experience and concept of the Goddess through fiction. Each one utilizes a type of trance writing and writes with the stated intent of reconstructing female identity. In order to understand the recurring themes that appear in this type of fiction, it is necessary to give a synopsis of the relevant theories of Helena P. Blavatsky, as her nineteenth-century construction of female divinity and occult science had a profound impact on subsequent Western esotericism; see chapter 1 for more on this.

Dion Fortune is the first twentieth-century author reviewed; her ideas were greatly influenced by Blavatsky's theories. Fortune is the one who came up with the original template for the fictional priestess, presented through the literary device of alternating third-person passages and first-person commentary, which is emulated by later authors. She incorporates theories from the Western Mystery Tradition and presents a dualistic concept of the Goddess, the White and Black Isis.

Marion Zimmer Bradley is the second author reviewed. She utilizes Fortune's original template and creates the society of Avalon, or college of priestesses. Bradley incorporates feminist spirituality and Christian esotericism into her ideal society, and she explicitly advocates the theory of the Triple Goddess, or Maiden, Mother, and Crone. However, there is some reference to a secret, fourth face of the Goddess, a dark and terrible aspect that is mentioned in her works.

Diana L. Paxson is the final author reviewed; after Bradley's death, she is continuing the Avalon series. She explores concepts of Heathenism and advocates a multifaceted image of the Goddess that is both transcendent and personal. Her priestesses often call upon the Dark Mother, who manifests as different versions of tribal deities who are personally connected to the land and priestess. The Dark Mother can also be considered an evolving fourth face of the Goddess or an extension of the priestess herself.

Each of the authors reviewed has a prolific amount of material and an esoteric philosophy that is distinct and, at times, contradictory to the others. A complete analysis of the separate philosophies of each author is beyond the scope of this work, but the reader is encouraged to do further research as inspired. Interested parties may prefer to read the fictional works prior to diving into this book, as there are many spoilers ahead. The focus of this project is the image of the priestess in esoteric fiction, primarily her commentary on sex and power from a female perspective. There is enough common ground between the three authors examined in *The Priestess and the Pen* to conclude that there is a literary lineage to the development of the priestess throughout twentieth-century fiction—and, by extension, to that of the Goddess.

Throughout the successive incarnations of the priestess reviewed, several themes remain constant. The priestess serves to remind people that there is a female component to the Divine, that sex is sacred, and that there are many ways open to women who wish to devote themselves to living in a sacred manner in a secular world. Sex can be both a destructive and a healing force. Women do not need to participate in a traditional family structure in order to serve their communities and have a positive influence on their cultures. Tradition is valid, but innovation is also necessary for spiritual evolution. Personal choice is a vital component in this process.

The Goddess has a mercurial nature. She is both light and dark, and she is eternal. She is transcendent but also capable of being contacted on a personal level. Her disposition is dependent on the personalities that invoke her. In order to achieve true power, one must acknowledge and submit to her. Although she is often depicted in human form, her motivations are unknowable to mortals. She has dominion over life and death. There is a numerical progression to the evolution of the Goddess throughout the texts. She is one and eternal; two, light and dark; three, Mother, Maiden, Crone; four, Dark Mother of Mystery. This fourth aspect is the most dynamic and open to interpretation. She can be the tribal or personal extension of the Goddess. She is the fairy queen, beautiful but poisonous. She is the killer, the womb that is the tomb. She claims the sword and wields it. In her dark aspect she is the Warrior, but when transmuted into her light form, she becomes the Lover.

Surveying the books, television shows, and motion pictures that are popular today, an interesting connection can be drawn between the images of women from the beginning of the twentieth century and those of the twenty-first century. Images of witches, sorceresses, and vampires abound, just as they did in the previous century, yet now they are presented from an entirely different angle. Instead of being used as anti-feminist propaganda, they have achieved mainstream status as depictions of female power. This change is the direct result of the concept of the priestess being introduced into popular culture through fiction. Referred to as mere wish fulfillment, historical romance, or gothic fantasy, this type of writing is often dismissed by scholarly research as less important than occult nonfiction to the growth of Neopaganism and related currents, and feminism in general. This is easily done, as the sexy details, colorful language, and controversial content do not translate into the politically correct neutrality that is favored by today's academic climate.

Yet these uncomfortable subjects are precisely why this type of writing is so important in assessing the rapid cultural change that has led to the rise of Western Goddess religion in the twentieth century. The dirty bits, the regressive attitudes, and the questionable language are what allow the reader to understand the cultural context of the time, to connect with the character and infer how the philosophies were interpreted and applied. These details also provide a glimpse of the personalities behind the stories and a key to understanding how women in the twentieth century have utilized these motifs to change common perceptions of female identity and create a new ideal. Cultural relevance is the component that the fiction supplies by incorporating factual details into the wider narrative. Finally, fiction provides a litmus test to gauge how far women have come in the goal of self-identification and whether they have been able to transcend the limitations of the past.

Based on the images that appear frequently in esoteric fiction, the results are mixed. While it is true that there are now many more positive female images available today, the tendency is still there to sort women into binary categories. Glinda stated it best: "Are you a good witch or a bad witch?" This dichotomy is demonstrated in esoteric fiction through the motifs of the priestess and the sorceress. The main distinction between the two is the utilization of sex and power. Both are premised on the concept of sex being a major component of a woman's power. One utilizes this power in service to her religion and tribe, honoring the traditional taboos of her caste and clan. The other uses this power in nontraditional ways but ultimately in the way that she deems most appropriate to her situation and that satisfies her personal needs. Depending on one's perspective and the circumstance, the lines separating the two become blurred. However, the endurance of these categories in esoteric fiction proves that there is considerable power in these labels on the female psyche. Regardless of whether these concepts originated as patriarchal labels, the tenacity of this dichotomy demonstrates that even in texts that promote Goddess-centered spirituality, the classic Madonna/Whore divide remains. Despite efforts to embrace female power as divine, female sexuality remains the source of feminine evil.

What can be concluded from the image of the priestess with the sword? This image has sustained over a hundred years of feminism, and consequently a century of new religious thought in the reconstruction of modern Goddess worship in the West. Stripped of its gender connotations, the sword represents authority. Ultimately, the woman with the sword is the woman with the pen; the one who wields it creates her reality. The strength of her vision becomes a conduit for others to expand their own realities. This interplay between the story and the audience promotes further experimentation with these ideas and, ultimately, a new gestalt.

In order to transcend the trap of patriarchy and biological dimorphism that limits all human potential regardless of gender, it is important to review the history of the visions and concepts that have paved the way for the present paradigm. This book is one attempt to categorize trends in the concept of the priestess—and, by extension, the Goddess—in fiction and esoteric theory from the modern era. The next step is to assess the strengths and weaknesses of the standard narrative in relation to one's personal experience. Finally, the most important part of the process is to develop a new narrative that includes one's authentic experience in combination with the wisdom of the past. This step is the most difficult, for it requires not only the abandonment of obviously flawed or harmful theory (such as spiritual racism) but also familiar motifs that may be comforting despite their limitations in favor of an entirely new language. This last part is crucial, for language fertilizes the mind, which conceives the future.

Another essential component in creating a new paradigm is audience participation, in which authors and readers meet in person to discuss new ideas and implement them within a social context. While the Internet is a wonderful tool for accessing information and making mental connections, in some ways it serves to isolate people from personal contact in favor of virtual interaction. This can be very educational, and the democratization of information has been a great boon, but personal introduction and interaction with like-minded folks is still the core element in affecting a rapid shift in cultural awareness.

One important facet in moving the current dialogue forward is to implement the lessons of previous pioneers. Review the current narrative. Play with reorganizing familiar concepts into new forms. Explore alternative philosophies, both to expose yourself to new stimuli but also to recognize what works for you. Utilize your voice and incorporate your personal experience. Exploit images of taboo into archetypes of power. Be bold. Write about your experiments, visions, theories, and share your results with others. Move beyond the mental realm, meet people, and create community. Most importantly, have fun. In order for Neopaganism and related philosophies to move beyond the limitations of biological determinism and to ensure a future that is relevant to the needs and experience of a wider populace, it is essential to formulate a new approach to the Divine that is less reliant on biological function and incorporates personal experience. Just as women maintain identities independent of their reproductive cycles, becoming someone other than another's daughter, mother, or grandmother, the concept of the Goddess must also evolve to embody new archetypes that symbolize an identity separate from her idealized biological function and reflective of the ultimate concerns and aspirations of her followers. For women in the West, these concerns include, but are not limited to, balancing career with family, reproductive rights, and bodily integrity.

What would the Goddess of the future resemble? In recent iconography, the priestess with the sword has transformed into the warrior woman. This change in perception reflects the concerns of the contemporary audience that she serves. The warrior woman embodies the metaphorical choice of "the baby or the blade." She represents working women, both those who have chosen to define themselves primarily through career and those who balance the challenges of work and family life. She is the champion of female equality in an ongoing gender war. She is both mercenary and clan-mother and, depending on her context, either solitary or group-oriented. By extension, the Warrior Goddess is self-determined, defined through her own independent action.

Unlike the facets of the Triple Goddess, the Warrior Goddess is not dependent on age, fertility, or caste. Women in any stage of their lives may embody this energy. The warrior and her converse image, the lover, both utilize the ancient source of female power, which is unbridled passion. Together they depict the concepts of Eros and Thanatos within the framework of a woman's experience. This experience is not always positive. The dynamic tension between the warrior and the lover creates a language women can use to discuss the success or failure of the ideal within their own lives. The positive benefits of exploring these motifs can only be gleaned after we acknowledge the darker realities they represent. Incorporating the warrior/lover into the dialogue forces us to look at the negative aspects of our culture and to question how the commodities of sex, violence, and endless war influence our lives.

Just as previous feminists mined images of perversity for constructions of power, the images of the warrior and lover will lend themselves to further examination and reinterpretation for generations to come. The next frontier in this dialogue is to reconcile the concept of woman as the killer with that of the lover and to discover who the idealized version of this woman would be The image of the Dark Mother is the harbinger of this type of exploration. She unifies previous paradox into an evolving archetype of increasing popularity and spiritual significance. As always, images of cultural taboo hold great power for those who are willing to study the symbols and unlock their potential. It is my hope that future writers will examine these motifs as sources of inspiration and have the courage to transmute these ideas into a new conversation with original characters that have yet to be written.

Chapter 1

WOMEN, LITERATURE, AND THE OCCULT IN THE MODERN ERA

DUE TO THE complexity of this topic, it is important to start with some context of the historical events, personalities, and theories that gave birth to the priestess in the modern era. This section begins with an overview of common terms used in this book, as well as a brief introduction of some of the occult organizations that have encouraged female participation. Speculative fiction, in the form of sci-fi and fantasy, is introduced as another forum in which women explore alternative constructions of female identity and power.

Definitions and Terms

This is a list of the terminology that will be used throughout this study, presented in a brief format for the ease of the reader. These are not rigid definitions but rather working terms to help organize my thoughts:

WESTERN ESOTERICISM. (The following definition is derived from the work of Antoine Faivre, who pioneered the academic research of occult history and philosophy.) A term used in religious studies to designate philosophies that encompass various subjects such as alchemy, astrology, magic, and theosophy, to name a few. A discourse dependent on a selection of relevant texts, specifically those of the Greco-Latin world from medieval to modern times that include the following characteristics:

Correspondence, or universal interdependence between all parts of the visible and invisible universe; the idea of the macrocosm and the microcosm, illustrated by the axiom "as above, so below."

Living nature. This is the idea that everything in nature is animated by hidden forces or energies that can be manipulated if one understands the harmonies inherent in correspondent signs.

Imagination and mediations. Utilizing the imagination to decode the symbols of the world through mediators that act as facilitators between the perceptible information and hidden concepts they represent. Anything or anyone that transmits the correspondent signs through symbolism is a mediator. Some examples are rituals, tarot, the Bible, angels, and initiators, or teachers who share the sacred system with their students or disciples.

Transmutation. This is the experience of gnosis, in which an illuminated knowledge is acquired through a process that is initiatic as well as visionary and occurs as result of a specific course of action. The participant is forever altered as a result of this experience.

Two additional characteristics that often enter the dialogue are:

The practice of concordance, in which several traditions are juxtaposed and studied in tandem in order to extract a *philosophia perennis*, or primordial tradition, from which all religions and esoteric traditions are derived.

The idea of transmission, whether from master to disciple or through initiation into a society. In order to truly participate in gnosis, a mediating third party must be present to facilitate the process.

OCCULTISM. A specific esoteric current which began in the mid-nineteenth century. Starting in France, it quickly caught on in Anglo-Saxon countries, influencing such groups as the Theosophical Society, the Hermetic Order of the Golden Dawn, New Thought, and eventually the New Age movement. The definitive factor of occultism is the return of an explicit discourse on magic, mainly absent in Western esotericism after the Enlightenment and Scientific Revolution. There is a strong focus on the occult sciences of magic, alchemy, and astrology. Occultism strives to merge all of Western esotericism into one organized tradition and reconcile scientific progress with esoteric wisdom, claiming there is no gap between science and magic.

NEOPAGANISM. An umbrella term that is used to delineate twentieth-century Paganism. It is an eclectic term that is inclusive of but not limited to the following examples: feminist witchcraft, religions based on science fiction, Heathenism,

Druidry, and Wicca. This term is used in religious studies to demarcate a specific philosophic current, or family of religious ideas. It is not intended to imply that the aforementioned currents are identical, but that they are related. (This is a strictly academic demarcation; I have yet to meet someone who identifies themselves as a Neopagan.)

THEOSOPHY. For the purposes of this book, this term will refer exclusively to the philosophy promoted by the Theosophical Society, established in 1875. Beginning from a theoretical basis that combines elements of spiritualism, Eastern mysticism, and Western esotericism, it was originally founded to conduct occult research and experimentation. Theosophy offered an alternative spirituality to people who were weary of the religion of the masses, as well as the materialism of science. It was based on a system of egalitarian fraternity and promoted the study of comparative religions and humankind's spiritual potential; it also popularized the idea that there is an underlying universal truth behind all of the world's religions.

ESOTERIC FICTION. A literary genre that presupposes a magical construction of the world in order to convey concepts of esoteric philosophy or alternative spirituality. It is an offshoot of magical realism, which is a genre that features magical elements or themes that occur within an otherwise mundane world. Esoteric fiction is related but begins with the opposite premise that the world is already enchanted and that mundane events occur in an otherwise magical universe. While this difference may seem slight, it presents a theoretical shift in the presentation of the literary content.

Women and Occultism

The Priestess and the Pen focuses on the literary character of the priestess in twentieth-century fiction. The authors reviewed were selected for their stated intention of utilizing this motif as a means of stimulating social consciousness to achieve a common goal of female empowerment and to introduce the concept of a female principle of the Divine, which activates an awareness in the readers who enjoy their stories.

Each author employs a specific literary technique for this purpose, an alternating first- and third-person dialogue with the reader. Utilizing this style for exposition of the story is an effective tool and is reminiscent of examples of trance writing dating from the nineteenth century. This type of writing, paired with the dynamic character of the priestess, is a potent combination that links alternative religions, feminism, and applied magic to social change.

In order to understand the evolution of this character throughout the twentieth century, it is important to revisit her origins and examine the connections between women, literature, and occultism at the end of the nineteenth century.

The nineteenth century was a time of rapid change in Western culture. The abolition of slavery, rapid scientific and technical advancement, and radical philosophies of the period were a potent combination for esoteric thought. Disenchantment in traditional religions and literal interpretations of the Bible spurred the growth of freethinking and alternative philosophies, which led to a time of unprecedented religious and social unrest. One specific category of esoteric thought that developed mid-century in France is that of occultism, which advocates the study and practical application of magic. The term came into common use after appearing in *Dogme et Rituel de la Haute Magie*, or *The Dogma and Ritual of High Magic* (1856) by Éliphas Lévi. It was introduced to the English-speaking world by H. P. Blavatsky in 1875.

Helena Petrovna Blavatsky is one of the most influential and controversial contributors to esoteric discourse from the nineteenth century. Born into a prominent family, she had access to private libraries and the means to travel worldwide from a very young age in search of esoteric truths and occult training. By her own account, she was sent to the United States with a mission to share spiritual truths she had acquired through study, travel, and direct transmission. She created the Theosophical Society with Colonel Henry Steel Olcott and George Henry Felt in New York City in 1875. Her theories on ancient mystery tradition, Eastern mysticism, Hermetic philosophy, and magic had an immense effect on Western esoteric discourse of the time. Her *Isis Unveiled*, a monumental work of 1,268 pages published in 1877, and *The Secret Doctrine* were tremendously popular and sold worldwide. She proposed that there was an ancient wisdom religion that could solve all discrepancies between science and theology. Posited as a sacred science, Blavatsky claimed that magic was the key to unification with the Divine and is at the heart of all major religions.

Blavatsky's theories of a universal occult tradition and her construction of spiritual evolution were eagerly embraced by an avid Western audience. Branches of the Theosophical Society were established throughout Europe, the United States, and India. An egalitarian organization, it encouraged members to participate through study, meetings, written discourse, and experimenta-

H. P. BLAVATSKY

tion. Even those who rejected the increasingly Eastern focus of her works and went on to establish societies with a distinctly Western focus—such as Anna Kingsford and Edward Maitland of the Hermetic Society and, later, the founders of the Hermetic Order of the Golden Dawn—still retained many of Blavatsky's most popular and controversial tenets. Blavatsky's example of a financially independent female occult philosopher, head of a huge international organization whose theories reached a worldwide audience, created an immediate response, as other women were similarly inspired to comment on these matters and propose their own Utopian ideals.

As a result, occult societies and periodicals, among the first organizations to welcome women as fully participating members, became fertile ground for early feminist thought. Joy Dixon traces the historical and political links between gender and esotericism in her book *Divine Feminine: Theosophy and Feminism in England*. In it she explores the relationship between the Theosophical Society and the women's suffrage movement, as well as the cultural milieu of the fin-de-siècle that encouraged ideological crossovers between early feminism and radical theologies:

> For at least a significant minority of women, feminism was a kind of theology as much as a political ideology. The current tendency to conflate political with secular makes it difficult to perceive the extent to which, in much of early twentieth-century feminist writing, the political realm was reconstituted as sacred space.[1]

Dixon states that while other studies have noted links between theosophy and the women's movement, they fail to sufficiently demonstrate the degree to which esoteric discourse was stimulated and modified through this interaction:

> The spiritual itself was a site of struggle; feminist versions of theosophy or esotericism existed in tension with other, often explicitly antifeminist interpretations of the esoteric tradition. Women's spirituality emerged from these struggles as a precarious, contradictory, and unstable formation; its mobilization within feminist political culture was also inflected by these struggles.[2]

Women were dominating the intellectual and political dialogue of the day, their theories inspired by their occult interests and per-

---

1 Dixon, 205.
2 Ibid., 6.

sonal experience. The idea of the preeminence of the divine feminine combined with the volume of new literature authored by women pioneered a new direction in Western history. This new era expressed itself in the politics and literature of the time.

Speculative Fiction and Religious Imagination

The literary trend of speculative fiction is another tool writers use to investigate radical alternatives to the dominant narrative and to reconstruct female identity. The literary genres of science fiction (sci-fi) and fantasy are fertile ground for this type of activity and have long been testing grounds that utilize symbolism and myth to explore alternative scenarios to the existing status quo. Science fiction often employs religious imagination in an effort to achieve some ambiguous truth, utilizing ideas of advanced technology and space and/or time travel as a metaphorical framework in which such theorizing can take place.

Typically science fiction is set in the future, utilizing advanced technology beyond what is presently available and incorporating themes of time travel, "psi" powers, and alien beings. Fantasy is often set in the legendary past or a similar alternate reality. Instead of technology, magical artifacts and powers are used to communicate with nonhuman beings that resemble those in folklore and mythology. These categories are not mutually exclusive and oftentimes explore common themes, albeit from a different theoretical framework.

Women pioneered this type of genre, beginning with Mary Shelley's *Frankenstein* in 1818, and have continued to challenge scientific and psychological assumptions of the human condition through their works. The fiction of Ursula K. Le Guin, specifically

The Left Hand of Darkness, published in 1969, is a prime example of this type of writing. Utilizing speculative fiction as a testing ground for new ideas, women have created a dialogue that challenges traditional stereotypes of womanhood. Science fiction of the pulp era (1929–1956) has many examples of theories proposing the inherent and necessary inequalities of gender, class, and race. Women are often portrayed as either voracious sexual creatures or damsels in distress. Outside of a few notable exceptions, such as C. L. Moore's *Jirel of Joiry*, women were largely excluded from being cast in leading roles. Instead, the female is often the monster the hero defeats or the prize to be won at the end of the quest. However, with the rise of second-wave feminism in the 1960s, speculative fiction was one area in which women could challenge the standard narrative of their times and discuss political and social reform through the voice of female characters.

One of these images is the idea of the heroic woman. A primary character, the female hero inspires and requires followers, and she is distinct from her sister the heroine, always a secondary role, who obeys. The woman hero defies the presumption that women are innately selfless, weak, or passive and in need of assistance from a male protagonist. This image of woman as hero is featured throughout contemporary sci-fi and fantasy, and she takes on a variety of forms. Often an author will take a negative concept and transmute it into one of autonomy and power: damsels become warriors, witches become wise women, sorceresses become priestesses. This fictional reconstruction parallels efforts made by women at the end of the Victorian Age to deconstruct the dominant narrative of inherent necessary inequality and create a new image of female empowerment.

Another element in twentieth-century speculative fiction that contributes to the spread of new ideas is the interaction of fans with authors through science-fiction conventions, or cons, as they are commonly called. Science-fiction fandom is a unique forum in which authors and readers congregate in order to discuss the themes and concepts popularized from the stories and to generally celebrate amongst peers. Much the same as esoteric societies, fandom provides a space for people to assemble with folks of similar interest and gives new writers a chance to connect with established authors and gain insight and tips on how to publish their own stories. Fandom also provides people the chance to debate topics popularized in the books by creating clubs in which readers connect and communicate with each other outside of the con, thereby creating an ongoing discourse that is both reflexive and interactive.

While connections between science fiction and new religions have been previously documented, as in the case of Scientology, there has been little research into the connections between speculative fiction and esoteric discourse. One of the goals of this book is to demonstrate how popular fiction has directly influenced the image of the priestess—and, by extension, the concept of the Goddess—in contemporary Neopaganism. This will be accomplished by examining works of speculative fiction that are examples of what will henceforth be referred to as esoteric fiction. This is fiction that deliberately incorporates occult themes and philosophy, written by authors who ascribe to an esoteric worldview and who present magic as a nomizing force in their fictional worlds. Esoteric fiction is most closely related to the literary genre of magical realism, but its unique elements justify its classification as a distinct subset worth independent research.

Fantasy versus Reality

One of the best ways to assess a culture is through its dreams and fears. Dreams reflect the hopes and aspirations of a society, if not its concrete reality. Fears and taboos are the ideas that both fascinate and terrorize the population they serve. Whether positive or negative, the fantasies of a culture demonstrate the universal concerns of their creators. Unfortunately, a common mistake that has plagued Western society is the confusion of theory with actual events, and this has led to social and scientific policies that have had disastrous consequences throughout the Victorian and modern eras. Observing conditions such as poverty, disease, and war, many theorists in the West have decided that there is an inevitability to human suffering, blending the societal ills of their time into their theories of bygone eras, concluding that the current state of affairs is ancient and inescapable. Mathematics, science, and philosophy have been used as a means to justify these claims, their arguments so compelling to the attitudes of the day that theories have been cherished as facts and continue to influence contemporary politics, as well as scientific and religious thought.

One work of particular interest to this topic is *On the Origin of Species*, authored by Charles Darwin and published in 1859. While proposing his theories on evolution, Darwin also included his assumptions about the inherent differences between male and female, and, utilizing social theories of his time, assigned certain traits to each sex, such as passivity for females, that continue to dominate evolutionary theory to this day. Darwin speculated about the nature of sexual evolution from prehistoric times, but his work is infused with Victorian gender politics and is transposed onto a mythical past. This controversial work was despised for its contention that evolution is a measurable, natural process instead of an act of God, but it was acclaimed for its assumptions about the biological determinism of human behavior.

This theory of biological determinism has served to enshrine the conflicted notions of Victorian womanhood and gave seeming scientific credence to the gender inequities of the time. Although Darwin himself pointed out that his ideas were only theories intended to speculate on the unknown causes behind observed phenomena, many people in the Western world embraced these concepts as immutable fact, and later scientists and philosophers thought up new applications of these concepts far beyond Darwin's stated purpose. Social Darwinism, eugenics, and evolutionary psychology all begin with a basic assumption of the truth of these ideas about the inherent qualities of the sexes. The concept of biological determinism easily segues into racial theorizing as well.

A redacted version of the standard narrative of Victorian sexuality posited women as reticent and coy, with limited libido. Compliant and completely dependent on the men in her life for emotional and financial security, the ideal woman had no independence whatsoever and existed to be the ideal wife and mother; family life was the sole focus of her attention. Denied the right to vote, study, and work on equal terms as their male counterparts, women at the end of the 1800s faced tremendous challenges and financial hardship existing outside of the traditional familial structure. The accepted narrative of the day produced extremely divergent conceptions of womanhood. On one end, women were objects of veneration, revered for their purity; on the other end, women were often construed as inherently deceitful, designed by God and nature to be seductresses, unable to control or deny these urges without male assistance. There was a strong division between the concept of the ideal "modest" woman, firmly located within a traditional family context, and the "immodest" woman, who inevitably fell into a life of degradation and prostitution. These extreme depictions, combined with increasingly restrictive social taboos, created a culture of sexual repression that continues to influence the contemporary standard narrative.

However, an increased interest in secular and religious humanism, combined with female participation in esoteric societies, gave rise to a very different construction of ideal womanhood. Embraced by feminists and feared by others, this new concept of radical female power is of key interest to this study, as it demonstrates the interplay of fantasy and reality in regards to female identity at the end of the nineteenth and beginning of the twentieth centuries. The recurrent images explored throughout the literature, art, and iconography of the time describe an enduring mythology of the destructive, catalytic powers of womankind.

Savior and Seductress

Nina Auerbach refers to this as the myth of the "Grand Woman," which emerged out of the Victorian imagination from a conflicting construction of woman as both victim and queen. The motif of the Grand Woman is very useful in analyzing the character of the fictional priestess, who often transitions between these extremes. Auerbach further subdivides this into "four central types: the angel, the demon, the old maid, and the fallen woman."[3] She postulates that this interpretation of the evolving myth of the feminine has particular cultural weight, as these constructions are independent of a woman's traditional equations with wife, mother, and daughter. This Grand Woman is a symbol of the magical, catalytic potential of these marginal areas of womanhood, unable to be fully controlled or understood by men. According to Auerbach, she demonstrates

> one way in which the decorous clash of cultures coalesced in a myth crowning the disobedient woman in her many guises as the heir of the ages and demonic savior of her race.[4]

Auerbach asserts that angels and demons were subject to a gender shift in Victorian iconography and literature, and unlike the "males with bisexual potential" that characterized the earlier works of Milton and Blake, images of angelic/demonic iconography became predominately female.[5] Angelic and demonic qualities become linked with magical powers attributed to women, and represent two extreme conceptions of womanhood that dominated the Victorian mind, neither one fully human. In the Victorian stereotype of the "Angel in the House," feminine angelic qualities manifest through domestic skill, dedication to family and hearth, and self-sacrifice. This female angel's mobility and

> strength of will and sheer physical stamina align her with an older angelology than our own stereotype of the moribund Victorian maiden has acknowledged.[6]

---

3   Auerbach, 63.
4   Ibid., 83.
5   Ibid., 74.
6   Ibid., 83.

Traditional angelic associations grant women a heroic fortitude in the face of adversity and a superhuman capacity for militant organization that distinguishes her from the rest of fallen humankind.

The female demonic is most often pictured or referred to as the mermaid, siren, or some other fantastic amalgam of woman and beast. Her hybrid nature and ambiguous classification symbolize the mysterious, unknown depths of feminine power in general and is symbolic of woman as the other—as non-humanity staring back in human form. The mermaid is the dangerous counterpart of the angel, for both possess an eternal beauty that is a core element of their power to transfigure and fascinate. In *Idols of Perversity* Bram Dijkstra asserts that images of mermaids and sirens are an attempt to artistically illustrate the antifeminist construction of the fearful yet alluring "New Woman" of the late nineteenth century. This was the term used to describe the emerging modern concept of female identity.

First popularized by the author Henry James, the term "New Woman" was used to describe the educated, independent career women of Europe and the United States and is synonymous with the suffragette movement, or first-wave feminism. At the close of the nineteenth century, women were entering the workforce and post-secondary education, producing female doctors, lawyers, and professors. This was an entirely new direction for Western society. In addition to economic independence, the New Woman also signaled a new era of sexual autonomy and legal authority for women, as many were granted property rights that were retained after divorce. This image of the New Woman was liberating for feminists and terrifying for those who were threatened by the social changes she embodied.

The New Woman refused to be molded in the image of the household nun:

> hence she personified the regressive, bestial element in woman's nature…The siren's physical allure spelled death to man's transcendent soul.[7]

The predatory mythology of the siren morphs directly into that of the vampire, which Dijkstra maintains is the dominant image of degenerative female sexuality of the twentieth century,[8] asserting that

> by 1900 the vampire had come to represent woman as the personification of everything negative that linked sex, ownership, and money.[9]

Like her aquatic sisters, the vampire's most effective weapon is her devastating beauty that turns men into her willing prey. Auerbach connects the poisonous beauty of the female vampire Carmilla and its hypnotizing affect on her victims with the pure beauty of the angel, noting that

> the shared motif of the eternal face shows that the angel can modulate almost imperceptibly into a demon, while retaining her aura of changelessness.[10]

---

7   Dijkstra, *Idols of Perversity*, 258–66.
8   Dijkstra, *Evil Sisters*, 3–7.
9   Dijkstra, *Idols of Perversity*, 351.
10 Auerbach, 107.

The categories of old maid and fallen woman are linked in this construction of Victorian myth, "each in her own way an exile from woman's conventional family-bound existence."[11] Representing the social reality of the breakdown of the family ideal, both figures are simultaneously pitied and feared. The relationship between these categories of womanhood parallels that of the angel/demon as embodiments of a woman's power, with the categories of spinster/whore also representing extreme ends of another female unknown, sex. Stripped of her demonic associations of witchcraft, the old maid assumes the qualities of a diminished angel in the service of a surrogate family. Without the familial constraints of Victorian life, the spinster also displays the angelic power of mobility and is free to travel alone, unhindered. Auerbach states that old maids are "often granted a shaping power ordinary fictional mothers and fathers do not have."[12] Her isolation becomes symbolic of self-sacrifice, and she becomes a spiritual paragon, distinct from her worldly sisters forever embroiled in the domestic chores of child-rearing and cleaning, free to concentrate on matters outside of the daily grind.

The fallen woman is the last category of the Grand Woman myth, as well as the most controversial. Just as the old maid is representative of the power of celibacy, the fallen woman symbolizes the dynamic, active power of sex. Choosing to "fall" empowers the woman to become "God of her world" through her subsequent actions after the event. Demeaned and exalted as both agent and victim in Victorian works, she encompasses "both the

---

11 Ibid., 162.
12 Ibid., 114.

pity of the woman's fall and the transforming power, not of her redemption but of her will to rise."[13] This catalytic power is symbolized by the moon in Auerbach's myth.

> Traditionally, it stands for changeableness, connoting not simply the wife's perfidy but the fallen woman's inherent power of metamorphosis which allows her to destroy and reconstruct her world.[14]

These four themes combine to illustrate the myth of the superhuman capabilities of woman independent of a maternal framework and are used by Mary K. Greer as an analytical template for the four main subjects of her biography *Women of the Golden Dawn: Rebels and Priestesses*.[15] They are included here to give the reader some of the cultural context of the images of women that were present at the turn of the last century as an alternative but pervasive artistic narrative that has had a direct effect on contemporary Western culture.

The Grand Woman is the daughter to the concept of the New Woman and is endowed with the superhuman, magical power to change herself and her world. Independent of conventional societal roles, she has the mobility, demonic knowledge, and superhuman will to accomplish this goal. This image is transformed into the priestess in the twentieth century.

---

13   Ibid., 188.
14   Ibid., 174.
15   Greer, 8–9, 16–17.

Chapter 2

DION FORTUNE/ VIOLET FIRTH

VIOLET FIRTH (1890–1946), writing under the pen name Dion Fortune, was a prolific author and lay psychologist. She was also an extensively trained ritual magician with an early interest in Christian mystical thought and extensive involvement in esoteric societies. Her interest in analytical psychology and occult studies began as the result of a psychic attack, which she defined as

> an application of hypnotic power to improper ends...The commonest form of psychic attack is that which proceeds from the ignorant or malignant mind of our fellow human beings.

Using telepathy or specific techniques, energies or entities can be consciously directed to cause psychic and physical harm to the victim.[16]

According to Fortune, her first employer, a formidable woman with "considerable knowledge of occultism obtained during a long residence in India," succeeded in hypnotizing Fortune when

---

16 Fortune, *Psychic Self-Defense*, xxv–7.

DION FORTUNE

she attempted to resign from her position. By repeating "You are incompetent, and you know it. You have no self-confidence, and you have got to admit it," the will of Violet Firth was successfully broken. Fortune recounts:

> My employer did not argue or abuse me. She kept on with these two statements, repeated like the responses of a litany. I entered her room at ten o'clock, and I left it at two. She must have said these two phrases several hundreds of times. I entered it a strong and healthy girl. I left it a mental and physical wreck and was ill for three years.[17]

Janine Chapman traces the date of the attack to April 1913.[18] This date is significant, for it was soon after this event that Fortune began to investigate the power and potential of the human mind,

---

17   Ibid., xvii–xxi.
18   Chapman, 172–180.

an interest that became her lifelong pursuit and characterized much of her personal philosophy and esoteric theory.

Raised as a Christian Scientist, she started exploring theosophy in 1914 and was initiated in 1924 into the London Christian Mystical Lodge; in 1919 she was initiated into the Hermetic Order of the Golden Dawn, and by 1922 she had founded the Fraternity of the Inner Light as an auxiliary branch of the Alpha et Omega temple. She began publishing ethical treatises as well as articles and books outlining her own interpretation and application of occult theories and techniques in 1926.[19]

Her prolific, provocative writings did not always make Fortune popular with her occult and theosophical contemporaries. Moina Mathers, widow of S. L. MacGregor Mathers and first fully initiated member of the Golden Dawn, was one famous example.[20] The two women disagreed about the content of Fortune's publications. Mathers was convinced that Fortune was out to publicize secret teachings of the Golden Dawn; Fortune retaliated publicly with essays outlining abuse in the occult world.[21] By 1928, due to conflict with Moina Mathers as well as strife within the Christian Mystical Lodge, Fortune left both esoteric societies and declared the Fraternity of Inner Light an independent order, fully functional as an initiatory tradition.[22] The works reviewed in this study are the product of Dion Fortune's "pagan period,"

---

19 Hutton, 181.
20 Greer, 56, 349.
21 Ibid., 357, and Fortune, "Ceremonial Magic Unveiled," 13–24.
22 Fanger, *Dictionary of Gnosis and Western Esotericism*, s.v. "Fortune, Dion."

as described by prominent Neopagan researcher Ronald Hutton, which lasted roughly from 1930–1939.[23]

Despite these accomplishments, a key component of Fortune's most popular writings is often overlooked by esoteric scholars and enthusiasts alike. While her fiction is acknowledged for its ritualistic content and emphasis on the magical potential of gender polarity, the novels are simultaneously dismissed as "overtly wish fulfillment fantasies, successful magical romances with gothic elements, and they continue to have a readership."[24] Ronald Hutton also cites the sex-based polarity theories and rituals in *The Sea Priestess* and *Moon Magic*, and the development of Fortune's construction of the Great Goddess as her most important and enduring contribution to modern Paganism, but undervalues the originality of her contribution by defining her spiritual growth and creative output primarily through her interaction with influential men in her life and translation of established theory.[25] Other researchers tend to present the concept of idealized spiritual marriage alongside the facts of her divorce in order to achieve an ironic effect:

> Her own marriage, though it seems in some respects to adhere to the basic plot outline discoverable in the novels (she and Evans spent years constructing a ritual space and doing magic together there), may have had less satisfying results from the perspective of wish fulfillment: having fallen in love with a younger woman, Evans petitioned for and was granted a divorce in 1939.[26]

---

23 Hutton, 188.
24 Fanger.
25 Hutton, 183–186.
26 Fanger.

Both Hutton and Fanger link this event, along with the loss of her longtime magical partner Charles Seymour, with the abrupt stop in her output of fictional work, and mention the outbreak of WWII almost incidentally; the implication being that her divorce was the more devastating development, her creativity crippled as her ideals of sacred marriage were destroyed. Alan Richardson also speculates about Fortune's state of mind and emotional health during this transitional period, characterizing her as "the Moon Priestess with no light of her own" and stating,

> Poor, poor Dion…what is she trying to tell us here, at the age of forty-five, when the menopause had begun, and her husband was more and more likely to leave as the days went by?[27]

Although the assertion that the end of her marriage coincided with a loss of fertility and spiritual focus may seem odd, this concept appears to be a popular theme among Fortune's biographers, with a few notable exceptions. Fortune's mental stability and creative output are frequently presented as being connected to and regulated by her hormones and ability to keep a husband. However, in a taped interview, two of Fortune's longtime associates, Evelyn Heathfield and Helah Fox, assert that Fortune's marriage to Penry "Merl" Evans ended amicably; Fox quotes Fortune as saying,

> Well, the time has come, and Merl has left. And that's the end…I feel it will be a shock to some people to know that this has happened, but it's just like a leaf withering and falling off.[28]

---

27   Richardson, 201.
28   Hapman, 84.

These do not appear to be the sentiments of a woman who is emotionally shattered by the termination of a relationship, so it is inaccurate to equate her divorce and cessation of fictional output with the terminus of her creative work.

> Despite what various commentators have said about Dion Fortune being a spent force, the fact is that late in the '30s, at the beginning of the war, it was Dion Fortune who remained firmly in control [of the Society of the Inner Light] and Colonel Seymour and Christine Campbell Thompson and Penry Evans who went.[29]

Academic disclaimers regarding the romantic elements of her novels abound, the repetitive plotline of female-to-male polarity magic dismissed as wish fulfillment because of her eventual divorce. This is an example of anecdotal bias on the part of the historian, as the actual details of Fortune's personal life have little relevance to the effect of her fiction on her readers. It is significant to note that historians rarely scrutinize the contributions of Fortune's male contemporaries through the details of their personal lives. Failed relationships, substance abuse, and other unsavory biographical details are often recounted in an anecdotal fashion but are typically presented separately from an analysis of their esoteric theory. Framing the cessation of Fortune's fictional output in terms of hormonal or emotional instability serves to disregard the intent of the author, who clearly arranges these elements for a specific goal. Fortune herself explains that the novels are meant to be read in tandem with her occult nonfiction:

---

29 Fielding and Collins, 148–149. Author's brackets.

> *The Mystical Qabalah* gives the theory, but the novels give the practice. Those who read the novels without having studied the *Qabalah* will get hints and a stimulus to the subconscious. Those who study the *Qabalah* without reading the novels will get an interesting intellectual jigsaw puzzle to play with; but those who study *The Mystical Qabalah* with the help of the novels get the keys of the Temple put into their hands.[30]

By her own account, the novels are intended to add an element that is not covered in her *Mystical Qabalah*, so isolating theories of the magical polarity as some of the most important components of the novels is not necessarily correct, as this information has already been introduced in her nonfiction work. Hutton makes the point that her other most notable contribution to contemporary Neopaganism is her construction of the Great Goddess as the primordial creatrix of all life, and credits the ritualistic content and poetic quality of the works as adequate explanation for their continued popularity.[31] I do not dispute this claim but respectfully suggest that the unique element of Fortune's fiction, the "keys of the Temple" she offers through her fiction, are themes that historians tend to discredit or ignore, namely the recurring plotline of esoteric romance told from the priestess's viewpoint.

This concept—an explicit discourse on sex and magic narrated from a female authority—is the most dynamic contribution that Fortune has made to Western esotericism. Presented as fiction, Fortune can discuss her personal experience and philosophy as a woman in search of the Goddess, attempting to rework a definition of female empowerment that is modern yet sacred. Her use

---

30 Fortune, foreword in *The Sea Priestess*, xiii.
31 Hutton, 186.

of repetition could be interpreted as an attempt to embed this idea into the minds of her readers, much the same way a hypnotist implants a suggestion in the mind of a client. Through fiction, her ideas of female empowerment and emancipation are disseminated to a far wider audience than the confines of a magical lodge or esoteric society. Rather than dismissing the repetitive plotline of her novels as some kind of failed personal fantasy, it may be more constructive to analyze Fortune's works in the spirit that the author presents them. The fiction is presented as a blueprint for putting esoteric theory and alternative spirituality into practice, with the woman directing the action. Her literary character of the priestess functions as an enduring template for generations of women to further experiment with these ideas, discussing their own theories of sex, power, and the Divine.

The archetypal importance Fortune assigns to this figure, along with the progressive shift of the narrator's gender from male to female and the catalytic, subconscious effect she attributes to this independent character, all demonstrate that the priestess is the key component in these texts. Fortune explains the process behind writing *Moon Magic* and the somewhat spontaneous development of Lilith le Fay as follows:

> It has been said that when a novelist imagines a situation he brings it to pass. Be that as it may, when I imagined the character of Vivien le Fay Morgan, or Lilith le Fay, as she variously calls herself, I brought into being a personality, and in the second book she figures the present volume—she is very far from being a puppet in my hands, but takes charge of the situation…After the conclusion of *The Sea Priestess* she would not lie quiet in her grave, but her ghost persisted in walking. It walked to such good purpose that it forced upon me the writing of this book. I had no clear idea of

the plot. Six times I started the book, and six times I scrapped the result, till finally the rejected chapters reached the dimensions of an average novel. Then finally I decided to tell the story in the first person, and Lilith le Fay took charge. I wrote it, in fact, to find out what it is about. I have put a great deal into it, and there is a great deal more than I have ever put in. One might even say that the writing of it was a magical act...I only know that Lilith lives after a curious manner of her own; she lives for others as well as for me; and it may well be that to some of those who read these pages she will come as a shadowy figure half-seen in the twilight of the mind.[32]

This type of writing, wherein the author takes on or speaks through a separate persona, is a type of trance writing that has been employed by female authors since the nineteenth century. According to Gilbert and Gubar, these types of "obsessive" or "involuntary" characters and motifs are some of the definitive characteristics of women's writing, in which a vision is worked out and reworked through prose.[33] Although Fortune's novels are produced in and firmly reflect the modern era, they are described as a type of trance writing by the author herself and are a determined effort to abolish regressive Victorian attitudes. The involuntary nature of Lilith le Fay, along with the successive retelling of her story throughout several volumes, disputes the idea that these novels are simply "wish fulfillment" and signifies that these works are a determined attempt to convey an alternative vision of woman as priestess and, ultimately, Goddess. Fortune's explanation that the exposition of this character's story as a magical act of mediumship is also significant, as this grants the text the

---

32 Fortune, "Preliminary Considerations" in *Moon Magic*, 10.
33 Gilbert and Gubar, 313.

status of a revealed text, or at the very least an exercise in automatic writing. Helena P. Blavatsky also claims a similar spiritual guidance from unseen "masters" who inspired her work. There could be other contributing factors to the cessation of Fortune's reworking of the priestess in fiction besides her divorce. The outbreak of WWII was not an insignificant event. Another likely scenario is that the consciousness that Fortune claims to have channeled in these stories stopped speaking once her story was told, as the message was transmitted and received.

In order to accurately assess the influence and contributions of Dion Fortune to contemporary religious movements, specifically those with a Goddess-centered spirituality, it is necessary to re-examine her literary character of the priestess and the effect that this concept has had on subsequent female authors who reinterpret this motif to explicate their own esoteric theories. The actual realization of these ideals in Fortune's personal life is less pertinent to the dialogue than the power of the fictional reality that she presents and its effect on her audience. By gendering the dialogue, Dion Fortune enables countless women to cast themselves in the role of the initiator and participate in a dynamic, radical religious experiment designed to reconnect humankind with the soul of nature and rediscover the divine Goddess. Fortune presents the character of the priestess as the terrestrial counterpart of this principle, describing two variations of the theme, Earth Mother and Moon Mistress.

Chapter 3

EARTH MOTHER/ MOON MISTRESS

THE THREE WORKS to be reviewed in this chapter are Dion Fortune's *The Goat Foot God*, *The Sea Priestess*, and *Moon Magic: Being the Memoirs of a Mistress of That Art*. All three novels are variations of a single plotline set in early twentieth-century England.

Each story begins with a male protagonist who is psychologically stunted or wounded and otherwise extremely dissatisfied with the circumstances of his life. He has an experience that signifies a break with his usual construction of reality. This break is triggered by an emotionally destabilizing event, such as the death of a spouse or a life-threatening illness, and is accompanied by seemingly unexplainable experiences that border on the paranormal, such as a disturbing sequence of dreams or visions.

A personality who is familiar with the elements of occultism is then introduced and proceeds to instruct and assist the protagonist in constructing a ritual space in which to enact a ritual drama that attempts to reunite the fractured portions of his psyche. This is accomplished through an invocation of the divine feminine, facilitated by the priestess. There is a noticeable progression and evolving complexity in Fortune's construction of the priestess that belies the simplicity of the unchanging plotline throughout the novels.

Two distinct categories of priestess emerge, as well as Fortune's definition of feminine evil. Priestess type 1, Earth Mother, makes her debut in *The Goat Foot God* (GFG) and reappears for a cameo in the final chapters of *The Sea Priestess* (SP). Type 2, Moon Mistress, is introduced in *The Sea Priestess* and dominates the narrative in *Moon Magic* (MM). Through her fiction, Fortune attempts to invest the divine, demonic powers of the feminine into an outlet that is socially acceptable and compatible. She does this with varying degrees of success, mainly due to the priestess's alien morality that is comprised of equal parts of Fortune's own syncretic religious beliefs, popular conceptions of feminine evil, and her provocative definition of modernity.

Priestess Type 1: Earth Mother

Earth Mother is Fortune's earliest model of the priestess and is arguably the most human, as both representations of her are women who grow into the role throughout the development of the story. While both priestess types require the masculine polarity to actualize her full potential, Earth Mother is completely complementary to the male priest and dependent on him for both her initiation into the mysteries as well as her continued participation in them, in essence to access her own power. Earth Mother's power, as her name implies, is derived from the inherent male to female polarity and the creative power of sex, attributed to the great god Pan throughout Fortune's works. The characters Mona

Wilkins of GFG and Molly Coke of SP conform to this pattern; their marriages at the end of the novels to their respective male protagonists cement their power and serve to sanctify Pagan ritual with a civil ceremony.

GFG begins by introducing Hugh Patson, who has just received the shocking news that his wife has been cheating on him with his cousin, and that both have been killed in a fatal automobile accident. Distraught, he stumbles into a bookshop and makes the acquaintance of Jelkes, proprietor of the establishment and later identified as a mediator of esoteric theory. Upon recognizing Hugh's unstable mental state, Jelkes invites Hugh to lodge with him for a while.

After an extended stay with Jelkes and exposure to some interesting books, Hugh decides to vacate his former demesnes and acquire a suitable place in which to embark on some practical occultism that incorporates Pagan elements. Hugh enlists Jelkes's help with the enterprise and entreats him to recruit an open-minded, artistic helpmeet (preferably female) to furnish and ornament the place as befits a temple and to participate in the rites. Mona Wilkins, "Designer and Craft-Worker," is introduced in the eighth chapter of GFG, and from her conversation with Jelkes about the nature of the job he has procured for her, it is clear that they know each other along "esoteric lines" and that this assignment includes a good deal more than the usual odd bit of interior decoration.

Throughout the course of refurbishing the derelict monastery that Hugh has acquired as a base of operations, his personality begins to fragment and blends with his alter ego, renegade medieval monk Ambrosius, who was executed for attempting to institute a Pagan worship at the same location centuries before. As Hugh's episodes increase in severity, Mona becomes instrumental in the attempt to repair Hugh's maligned masculinity and fractured sense of self. She takes part in a reenactment of the invocation of the Pagan god Pan that Ambrosius was unable to complete, and the experiment is a success. Consequently, Hugh falls in love with Mona. While Mona is not overtly interested in Hugh, she is fascinated by the tormented and passionate Ambrosius. The denouement of the piece is the moment when Hugh fully integrates Ambrosius into his personality and finally succeeds in seducing Mona.

Businesslike and professional, Mona epitomizes her creator's first prototype of modern womanhood: incorporating the magical elements of the angel/demon with the independence and sexual knowledge of the old maid/fallen woman. Described as possessing a "Bohemian soul," Mona has lived the life of a girl artist and is sexually experienced. From the very first meeting with Hugh, she is portrayed as knowledgeable about the religion of the Old Gods, and she instructs him on the selection and preparation of the temple location. When questioned about her introduction to esoteric Paganism, Mona reveals that Jelkes was actually the first to suggest she explore these concepts, although it is implied that Mona has now surpassed her teacher by virtue of being less repressed than her aged instructor. Modernity equates to being morally and sexually unrepressed, and Mona's attitude throughout the text summarizes Fortune's solution to sexual repression, which is a revival of Paganism.[34] This sentiment is best expressed

---

34 GFG 372.

by Mona herself when questioned by Jelkes as to why she does not immediately respond to Hugh's suit:

> "You could make him a good wife if you made up your mind to it."
> "Oh no, I couldn't. I am not the stuff of which good wives are made. I'd be a top-hole mistress to the right kind of man, but I'd be a domestic fiend to the wrong one."

This exchange demonstrates that the locus of Earth Mother's power is very close to that of the fallen woman and the demon, as it is reliant on the taboo of independent female sexuality. The mutability and willfulness associated with these stereotypes has been transformed into an authentic source of feminine power, as Mona uses them to positively identify herself. Shocked, Jelkes accuses Mona of being an "immoral young woman." Mona refuses this label by replying,

> "On the contrary, I am exceedingly moral. If I were what you say I am, I'd marry Hugh, and do him down, and clear out on the alimony."[35]

This passage illustrates that the priestess ascribes to a unique moral code, alien to what is endorsed by conventional standards but fundamental to Fortune's vision of female empowerment.

Earth Mother has the angelic power to renew and refresh the souls of men, yet her methods utilize the demonic powers of the sexual woman. Earth Mother may marry her priestly counterpart or not, as she chooses. This is important, as it is the first introduction of Fortune's ideals regarding the priestess's sexual ethics.

---

35 Ibid., 324.

Mona Wilkins may not be proper by the conventional standards of her time, but she is at least intellectually honest and decent enough not to use Hugh's feelings for her against him to dive into his wallet. Earth Mother has a place within the domestic paradigm, but she is not necessarily a wife or physical mother. She uses the creative power of sex to inspire, heal, and manifest the female divine. She is modern in that her concept of sacred sexuality is not dependent and sanctified solely through marriage, and she is an independent agent. She operates by undoing the emotional and psychic trauma of the men she works with, utilizing her knowledge of the magical potential of sex as a healing force.

While the plotline is primarily an esoteric Bildungsroman, Fortune also makes a political statement about gender roles of her time, proposing an esoteric alternative and role reversal. The use of a male narrator to convey this message is significant within the paradigm of women's writing. According to Gilbert and Gubar,

> many women working in a male-dominated literary tradition at first attempt to resolve the ambiguities of their situation not merely by male mimicry but by some kind of metaphorical male impersonation. [This allows the female author to] gain male power, not only to punish her own forbidden fantasies but also to act them out.[36]

The transition of the narrator from male to female in Fortune's recurring plotline accentuates the increasing emphasis on the character of the priestess. This marks a distinct transition in her work between using a male mediator to convey her occult

---

36   Gilbert and Gubar, 316.

philosophies and later presenting her theories as originating from a female source.

Through her recurring plot structure and successive male characters, Fortune asserts that it is only through submission to the female principle embodied by the priestess that the "cosmic forces" of the universe can be put back into balance. The spiritual despair that she sees characterizing the modern condition can be repaired through reconstruction of the ritual and the correct invocation of these forces into their human counterparts. Both sexes are necessary to induce the right type of conditions for this power to manifest itself. This motif is illustrated by Hugh's realization in GFG:

> He could go no further. He lacked his priestess. The power that had sought expression through him could find no passage, for the circuit did not lead to earth but remained insulated in empty space.[37]

This is echoed through similar sentiment expressed by Wilfred Maxwell of SP and Rupert Malcolm in MM.[38]

Fortune attempts to counterbalance this submission by stressing the indispensable role of the male as priest-initiator throughout all of the works, but increasingly weaker versions of the male characters are presented, whereas the image of the priestess gains complexity. This increasing emphasis on the priestess's role as initiator, combined with the invocations of female deity that characterize the magical rituals of the last two novels, reveal a shift in the author's focus. These changes reflect the primacy of the

---

37 GFG 351.
38 SP 219–220, and MM 228.

woman and her role in the manifestation of the Goddess. Earth Mother is presented as a modern woman who is conscious of her power, sexually experienced, and knowledgeable of her link to the Divine. Although Earth Mother is knowledgeable of esoteric forces and can construct a basic ritual, her full potential is only realized through continued interaction with the male protagonist, as evidenced through the marriage of the characters at the end of two of the novels. In this way, the priestess is still dependent upon men for her spiritual progress. In later novels, Fortune further refines her concept of the priestess by proposing a model that is unencumbered by terrestrial concerns and firmly located outside of the traditional concepts of wife and mother.

Priestess Type 2: Moon Mistress

Priestess type 2 makes her debut in SP and resurfaces to dominate the narrative in MM. The primary difference between her character and that of priestess type 1 is that whereas Earth Mother is a symbol of fecundity and, as her name attests, necessarily engages in sexual relations with her priest, Moon Mistress is sterile and, for the most part, celibate (although not virginal), instead concentrating her creative powers on occult matters and the finding and training of new priests. Priestess type 2 expresses her views on sex in MM, summarizing her unique morality and ultimate purpose:

> Why should I reproduce my race before or after my prime? Why should I, in fact, reproduce it at all in a densely populated country if I have other contributions to make to the common welfare? Distinguish, like the Greeks did, between sex for reproduction and sex for happiness, and I think you have the key. I, for my part, am a free woman and a priestess of the most ancient gods—that gives you the key to me.

> [Also,] I shall never give life on the physical plane; all moon priestesses must be sterile, that is why I will not marry, there is no purpose in it. My work is on the inner planes and concerns the life of the race.[39]

This freedom from domestic responsibility allows her more time, an increased focus on her magical tasks, and the ability to manipulate subtler energies than those available to Earth Mother. It also connotes a higher grade of initiation than her earthly predecessor. Moon Mistress combines the powers of the angel/demon with the independence of the spinster/whore.

Priestess type 2 is characterized in both texts by Vivien/Lilith le Fay Morgan, reincarnated magician and priestess, approximately 120 years of age. Unlike Earth Mother, Moon Mistress is introduced in the texts as fully trained and knowledgeable of her task from the beginning. She personifies many of Fortune's beliefs on reincarnation, as well as her speculations of the link between British Paganism and the mystery religion of the legendary lost continent of Atlantis. While there is the suggestion of a possible past-life connection in ancient Greece between Mona and Hugh (GFG 127), the text also suggests that this could be a subliminal wish-fulfillment fantasy on Hugh's part.

However, this past-life connection to the Atlantean priesthood is an explicit plot modifier in the subsequent two novels, as both of the men le Fay instructs have committed some kind of sexual or religious transgression with or against her in a past life, and a central component of their training is the recognition and expiation of these former sins, which are intimately connected with

---

39   MM 150, 207.

the circumstances of their current incarnations.[40] (The Atlantean theme is picked up later by Marion Zimmer Bradley to explore in her *Fall of Atlantis* and Avalon novels.) Both novels adhere to the basic plot template outlined earlier, with Wilfred Maxwell of SP and Rupert Malcolm of MM cast into the role of emasculated protagonists in need of spiritual and psychological healing that can only be achieved through ritual drama and interaction with the divine feminine that is personified by the priestess as the initiator.

While the role of the priestess in all of the works involves the psychological reconstruction of the male protagonists, Moon Mistress deliberately invokes and manipulates the sexual tension that Earth Mother attempts to balance out and mitigate, bringing it to a fever pitch. The goal is to heal the wounded psyche of the priests through deliberate application of the heightened energies of the pair. This technique is not without risk to the participants, as le Fay explains to both men before the most intensive workings; the possibility of them suffering a complete nervous breakdown is

---

40 Wilfred Maxwell is revealed, though dreams and divination, to have been a chosen sacrifice whose undeniable last request is to have sex with the priestess who conducts the rite, thereby breaking the sexual taboos of the priestly Atlantean caste. His physical condition of asthma is connected to his death by drowning in the previous incarnation (SP 111–116). Rupert Malcolm believes that he infiltrated the Atlantean priesthood in a former incarnation and became outcast when discovered by being assigned the role of sacrificial priest. Matters become further complicated through an illicit love affair with a priestess and his desecration of her corpse, which leads to his execution by torture; these events are determined to be the root of his horror of blood and the loveless marriage that dominate his current incarnation (MM 130–131).

high. She offers both men the option to quit if they feel unable to complete the transformation.[41] Although she retains her celibate stance throughout all of *Sea Priestess*, as the intensity of the magical working and the psychological problems of Rupert Malcolm prove to become more extreme than in the previous scenario, physical sex is explained as the final "safety valve" available in the event of an emergency, a last resort that would end the magic but effectively prevent a state of mental imbalance in the priest.[42]

The use of sex as an esoteric fail-safe against nervous breakdown shows Fortune's modern approach toward practical occultism and is a key component to her development of the priestess. The priestess is the woman who knows the secret function of sex and how it connects us to the Divine. Her role is to use this power to heal and to propel the spiritual development of her culture. She is the living link between man and the Goddess, for he can only achieve balance through interaction with her and submission to the female principle she embodies. Freed from the constraints and obligations of domestic life, the sexuality of the priestess is used to achieve something besides procreation; instead, it is offered as a sacrament to connect her partner with the Divine.

White versus Black Isis

Fortune's construction of the Goddess is central to her fiction, and it is important to note how she inverts traditional images and iconography to describe her concept of the female divinity. Traditional associations of womanhood glorify ideals of female passivity and submission; Fortune reinterprets these tropes to signify a

---

41 SP 130 and MM 115, 210.
42 MM 211.

subtle yet active power inherent to the female principle in a sexually dimorphic universe. Fortune similarly subverts other traditionally limiting symbols of female submission into ones of feminine power and dynamism. Two such images that Fortune employs to this end are the color white and the veil; her reinterpretation of these themes is the basis of her archetypal Goddess, Isis. Whereas Helena P. Blavatsky previously introduced the concept of Isis and female divinity to a Western audience, Dion Fortune refines this concept by presenting a dualistic concept of Isis as both black and white.

The color white has traditional associations of virginity, purity, innocence, passivity, and female vulnerability; it is most often associated with the angel motif of Victorian iconography, often depicted as clothed in white.

> In its absence of color, her childish white dress is a blank page that asks to be written on just as her virginity asks to be "taken," "despoiled," "deflowered."[43]

Throughout the nineteenth century, white is also associated with ghosts and the supernatural, and it has the ability to transform from an angelic quality to a demonic one. Representative of brides and corpses, the color white symbolizes the conflicting and extreme constructions of womanhood that dominated the Victorian age.

As the white dress can be considered indicative of the conflicting demands of society imposed upon women, the veil is symbolic of both a renunciation and acceptance of these demands. The veil has traditionally been regarded as a uniquely feminine

---

43 Gilbert and Gubar, 616.

symbol "because it is the woman who exists behind the veil in patriarchal society, inhabiting a private sphere invisible to public view."[44] An ambiguous symbol, the veil resembles a wall, but its transparency transforms it into a possible entrance or exit:

> Unlike a door, which is either open or shut, however, it is always potentially both—always holding out the mystery of immanent revelation, the promise or the threat that one might be able to see, hear, or even feel through the veil which separates two distinct spheres: the phenomenal and the noumenal; culture and nature; two consciousnesses; life and death; public appearance and private reality; conscious and unconscious impulses; past and present, present and future.[45]

Fortune uses the images of whiteness and veils to construct an alternative route to female empowerment that does not require the acceptance and assimilation of patriarchal interpretations of these motifs. Fortune rejects the stultifying power of white in many of her novels by dressing her priestesses in bold, vivid colors and invoking her Goddess under the name of Black Isis:

> Great Isis built up, the terrible Black Isis, the source of all power, who seldom comes, and only at the great moments. I am used to Her power and received it fearlessly, knowing that in a few seconds She would change into Her beautiful aspect, which is so much more beautiful than anything that can be built under the symbolism of the White Isis, who is always liable to change over into the Black Isis if too much power is brought through Her. Therefore we who have knowledge work with the Black Isis and transmute Her.[46]

---

44 Ibid., 474.
45 Ibid., 468–469.
46 MM 88.

This passage is a metaphorical renunciation of all of the associations the color white has assumed for women in literature, both of the white dress of virginity and the white shroud of death. Fortune instead embraces the color black as a symbol of fecundity and dynamic power as opposed to the eternal sterility of white, thereby stepping outside of the confines of literary symbolism altogether by inventing her own symbolism and assigning her own meaning. These ruminations on the nature of the Goddess, both light and dark, are tantalizing in their obscurity and inspire later writers to pick up and expand upon these themes.

Likewise, the symbol of the veil employed in Fortune's works is not one of modesty or renunciation; instead, it is the veil of mystery that shrouds the sacred image of the Goddess, shielding her from the sight of the profane:

> I am the veiled Isis of the shadows of the sanctuary. I am she that moveth as a shadow behind the tides of death and birth. I am she that cometh forth by night and no man seeth my face. I am older than time and forgotten of the gods. No man may look upon my face and live, for in the hour he parteth my veil, he dieth.[47]

Death in this context is not the physical death of one who gazes upon Medusa, but rather the spiritual death of initiation that simultaneously implies a spiritual rebirth and renewal.[48] Parting the veil is therefore a metaphor for accepting the female in her entirety and an acknowledgment of both her sacred and sensual aspects. The priestess, as the reflection and conduit of Black Isis, the Great Goddess, is also representative of Fortune's concept of

---

47 Ibid., 154.
48 Ibid., 155.

idealized womanhood; this theme is constantly restated throughout Fortune's fictional works but is best summarized in the following passage:

> Our conventions have so stereotyped the polarity between a man and a woman that it has got stuck and no one knows how to shift it. But what we want in the part of marriage that is behind the veil is the dynamic woman, who comes in the name of the Great Goddess, conscious of her priesthood and proud of her power, and it is this self-confidence that the modest woman lacks.[49]

As either Earth Mother or Moon Mistress, Fortune's priestess is a concentrated effort on the part of her author to challenge the standard narrative of sexual politics of her time, introduced through the vehicle of fiction. Using fiction, Fortune is able to engage in an explicit dialogue about sex and power that is not bound to the authorial restraint necessary for a nonfictional work. The exposition of her novels is that of an intimate memoir. It is this passion that distinguishes Fortune's fiction from her nonfiction because it frames esoteric dialogue in a manner that is anything but neutral, dry, or academic. It is for this reason that the character of the priestess should be considered as Fortune's key innovation and contribution to Western esotericism, as this character is the vehicle for her most arresting Goddess images and independent occult theories.

---

49 SP 219.

Chapter 4

MARION ZIMMER BRADLEY

MARION ZIMMER BRADLEY was born June 3, 1930, on a farm east of Albany, New York. The first of three children, she grew up during the Great Depression and WWII. As a young woman she exhibited signs of a strange ailment, possibly undiagnosed rheumatic fever, which kept her bedridden for several months before her seventeenth birthday, to which she contributed her lifelong atypical arthritic symptoms.[50] A precocious learner, she graduated high school three weeks after her sixteenth birthday, and after reading *Startling Stories* in August 1946, she began attending science-fiction conventions. She then published a fanzine, or amateur magazine, for science-fiction fans.

Between September 1946 and February 1949 she attended the New York State College for Teachers; in October 1949 she married Robert A. Bradley. After the birth of her first child in 1950, the family relocated to a small town in Texas with a population of 650 inhabitants. According to her biographer, her experience with the inhabitants of her new home caused her to reject orthodox

---

50   Arbur, *Marion Zimmer Bradley*, 30.

MARION ZIMMER BRADLEY

Christianity and conservative religion.[51] One assumes that this is a discreet reference to the beginning of Bradley's fascination with occultism and alternative religion, specifically feminist spirituality. Despite this statement, Bradley claims Catholicism in later interviews when questioned about religion and avoids being labeled as a Pagan or a priestess in print.

Throughout the end of the 1950s and through the mid '60s, Bradley began writing speculative fiction about the planet Darkover, inhabited by a lost colony of Earth that has acutely developed psi powers and is organized as a quasi-medieval society. Concurrently, she wrote several lesbian pulp novels under various pen

---

51   Ibid., 31.

names and was a regular contributor to *The Ladder*, which was a periodical produced by the Daughters of Bilitis, the first lesbian civil and political rights activist group in the United States. While attending Hardin-Simmons University in the early 1960s she separated from her husband and met Walter Breen in 1962. By 1963 she graduated with a triple major in English, educational psychology, and Spanish literature. Moving to Berkeley, she was granted a divorce from Robert Bradley in 1964, whereupon she immediately married Breen, and they had two children. However, she retained the name Bradley as she had attained a substantial science-fiction following as an avid participant and early supporter of sci-fi fandom.[52]

The Darkover novels proved to be fertile ground for her exploration of psychological and societal issues. Two novels of particular interest are her *Thendara House* and *City of Sorcery*, which contain the esoteric themes and her prototype for the college of priestesses found later in *The Mists of Avalon*. Although Bradley emphatically disassociates herself from feminism, her fiction is often characterized by themes of female self-determination and power. Bradley's refusal to label herself as a feminist is indicative of her determination to avoid being pigeonholed; instead, she used her fiction to challenge the female stereotypes of her time. This is clear from her reluctance to publicly describe herself as a lesbian or as a Neopagan throughout her life. However,

---

[52] Bradley and Breen separated households in 1979 and were divorced in 1990 after Walter Breen was convicted of child molestation. In 2014, Moina Greyland, daughter of Walter Breen and Marion Zimmer Bradley, released an online statement accusing her mother of sexually abusing her as a child.

since themes of sexual and gender identity, esotericism, and Goddess-centered spirituality dominate her fiction, and she has successfully promoted other authors that work with similar concepts, her image of the priestess is vital to the contemporary discussion of the ideal woman in an esoteric context.

Her most famous work, *The Mists of Avalon*, is a reconstruction of Arthurian myth told from the perspective of Morgaine, Bradley's version of Morgan le Fay. In Bradley's work, Morgaine is not portrayed as an evil sorceress but as a priestess of the original matriarchal religion of the British Isles, whose customs and way of life are fast disappearing with the rise of patriarchal Christianity. Kristina Hildebrand states that as

> part of the emerging Neopagan religious tradition, Bradley's text both explores and promotes it; the pre-Christian religion of Goddess worship being represented as the same as modern Goddess worship is part of this promotion.[53]

This is a valid observation and is precisely what Dion Fortune's fiction did fifty years earlier for the Western Mystery Tradition when she speculated that the occult rituals in her books were the vestiges of ancient Atlantean wisdom. However, Bradley's opus was of such a broad scope that it appealed to a much wider audience than Fortune's fiction ever did. Consequently, Bradley brought concepts of Western esotericism to the mainstream public, which became tremendously popular translated through her unique lens. Bradley recounts her own reasons for writing *Mists*:

> For me the key to "female personality development" in my revisionist, or better, reconstructionist version, is simply this. Modern

---

53 Hildebrand, 112.

> women have been reared on myths/legends/hero tales in which the men do the important things and the women stand by and watch and admire but keep their hands off. Restoring Morgan and the Lady of the Lake to real, integral movers in the drama is, I think, of supreme importance in the religious and psychological development of women in our day.
>
> I feel strongly that it has been a genuine religious experience. About the time I began work on the Morgan le Fay story that later became *Mists*, a religious search of many years culminated in my accepting ordination in one of the Gnostic Catholic churches as a priest. Since the appearance of the novel, many women have consulted me about this, feeling that the awareness of the Goddess has expanded their own religious consciousness, and ask me if it can be reconciled with Christianity. I do feel very strongly, not only that it can, but that it must.[54]

The sentiment expressed by the above passage clearly indicates Bradley's indebtedness to Fortune for both literary style and esoteric theory. Like Fortune, Bradley emphasizes the character development of the priestess as the necessary component to this empowerment of women and seeks to reconcile Christianity with contemporary identity by proposing Goddess worship as an alternative narrative, told from a position of female authority. Using a fictional retelling of an ancient myth allows Bradley to express views that would be untenable in any other forum, and disseminates her favored esoteric concepts and philosophy of womanhood to an even wider audience than her predecessor, as she had already established a significant fan base through her previous works. It also allows Bradley to engage in the explicit dialogue about sex, magic, and the role of the priestess begun by Fortune

---

54 MZB, "Thoughts on Avalon," http://mzbworks.home.att.net/thoughts.htm.

in the 1930s, updating it with the contemporary concerns of her time.

Diana Paxson, Bradley's editor and contemporary, confirms Bradley's esoteric background as a corollary and explanation for the themes discussed in *The Mists of Avalon* and related works, citing Fortune as a direct influence on Bradley's personal spiritual practice and writing style. Bradley explores her version of the esoteric Arthurian mythology proposed by Fortune throughout her works, particularly *Avalon of the Heart*. She also utilizes the stylistic device of alternating passages written in the third person with the first-person commentary of the priestess throughout the text.

This powerful technique draws the reader into the narrator's inner monologue. The information shared is hidden from the other characters in the text, as the priestess speaks plainly of internal conflicts and mistakes that influence the course of events in the story. This device is utilized throughout the Avalon series and gives each incarnation of the priestess a chance to tell her personal experience within the wider context of the narrative.

The complete Avalon series is a combined effort of Marion Zimmer Bradley and Diana L. Paxson to explicate Dion Fortune's concept of an esoteric link between Atlantis and the British Isles, as well as a means to describe each author's distinct approach to Goddess worship, interweaving the story of the original matriarchal religion of the British Isles with historic events and proposing an alternative explanation of history and religion.

Another major influence on Bradley's fiction came from her participation in Darkmoon Circle, a Goddess-centered feminist spirituality group that became the model for the college of priestesses in *Mists* and provided the Neopagan format of the rituals of the Goddess religion. While Darkmoon Circle continued to meet throughout the seventies, Bradley was eventually consecrated both as a Priestess of the Goddess and later as a Priest in the Pre-Nicene Gnostic Catholic Church. Breen and Bradley separated households in 1979 and were officially divorced in 1990. In 1981, Marion Zimmer Bradley, Elizabeth Waters, and Diana L. Paxson incorporated the Center for Non-Traditional Religion (CNTR) to host Pagan rituals, the ceremonies of the AOR (Aquarian Order of the Restoration), and services of the Pre-Nicene Gnostic Catholic Church. The Pre-Nicene Gnostic Church was established in 1952 by Australian-born Ronald Powell and is an offshoot branch of the Liberal Catholic Church (LCC), founded in 1916 in Sydney by James Ingall Wedgwood and Charles Webster Leadbeater, two of the most prominent and notorious members of the Theosophical Society, who strove to blend theosophical mysticism and Catholic sacramentalism.[55] *The Mists of Avalon* was published in 1982 and contains many of these alternative religious philosophies.

A prolific author with more than one hundred fictional and nonfictional works, Marion Zimmer Bradley died on September 25, 1999, in Berkeley, California, four days after suffering a major heart attack. Many of her unfinished literary projects have been taken up by her friends and protégés, and works co-authored by Bradley continue to be published to this day. Two examples are her Avalon series, continued through supplementary writings of Diana L. Paxson, as well as the Sword and Sorceress series, now edited by Elisabeth Waters.

---

55 Dixon, 84.

Bradley wields significant literary influence as a result of her numerous editorial projects and magazines, which feature stories of women as protagonists and heroes. Her Sword and Sorceress anthology is of particular interest, as it continues to be a forum for new authors to reinterpret gender roles and power. Bradley stated her goal for the series as follows:

> Valor has neither race nor color—nor does it have gender. That I have chosen stories mostly about women is a personal preference—not a prejudice. That I have chosen stories about both men and women, is, I hope, a sign of the times, and a hopeful outlook for the future of heroic fiction. And, since life always imitates art, it may be a heroic sign of the future of both women and men. Anyone can write male sexist fiction: anyone can write feminist propaganda. I hope to avoid both, and to entertain you while I'm doing it.[56]

Greyhaven is an anthology compiled of stories submitted from Bradley's close friends and family. The current residence of Diana L. Paxson, Greyhaven began as the residence of Marion Zimmer Bradley and her two brothers. Both brothers soon married, and as a result of their combined effort and the introduction of numerous friends and colleagues, a literary gestalt was born:

> On a purely physical level, Greyhaven is a huge, grey-shingled house in the Claremont district of the Berkeley hills. On a subtler level, it is a household, an extended family, a state of mind. On still another level, it is the center on a circle, a literary school of writers, both in Berkeley and through the world of fantasy and science fiction...Time went on. Children were born to all three marriages. The family outgrew even the enormous house called Greyhaven, and established House Greenwalls. Through the two

---

56   MZB, introduction in *Sword and Sorceress*, vol. 1, 13.

households passed a great number of young people—as friends, visitors, babysitters and what have you—and since like attracts like, a large number of these people passing through turned out also to be aspiring writers, who were given houseroom, and even more importantly, writing space, use of typewriters, encouragement, and the company of their peers.[57]

Several authors, such as Jennifer Roberson and Mercedes Lackey, became famous after being promoted and published in a Bradley collection and could be considered writers of the Greyhaven school. In addition to providing a physical space as well as a fictional forum that facilitated speculative writing, Greyhaven also contributed to the development of the Society for Creative Anachronism, or the SCA, and Bradley is credited with coining the name of the group. Founded in 1966, the SCA grew out of a science-fiction and fantasy theme party organized by Paxson into an international society dedicated to the selective recreation of medieval arts and culture from approximately 600–1600 CE. As a not-for-profit educational organization, the SCA includes more than 30,000 paying members in the US, Canada, United Kingdom, Sweden, Finland, Germany, Italy, Greece, Romania, Japan, New Zealand, South Africa, and Australia.

Marion Zimmer Bradley was posthumously awarded the World Fantasy Award for lifetime achievement in 2000. In 2001, Bradley's *The Mists of Avalon* was made into a televised miniseries directed by Uri Edel. Hutton summarizes the importance of Bradley's *Mists of Avalon* to Neopaganism witchcraft with one sentence:

---

57 MZB, introduction to Greyhaven, http://www.grendelheim.com/greyhaven/history.htm.

A remarkable and thorough reworking of the classic British epic, the Arthurian legends, it presented a huge reading public—on both sides of the Atlantic—with the concept of witchcraft as the Old Religion, integrally associated with female power and suppressed by a patriarchal and puritanical Christianity.[58]

Although Hutton primarily mentions *Mists* as a supreme example of the larger witchcraft trend that characterizes the late 1970s and early 1980s, his anecdote of one woman's conversion to witchcraft succinctly illustrates the purpose of this book:

> The bus actually takes her to France, where she finds work harvesting crops, and meets and joins people with socially and politically radical ideas. Through them she enters activist politics, encounters ideas of feminist witchcraft, and reads *The Mists of Avalon*. Now, Lesley doesn't know much about the history of witchcraft, but she has a very shrewd suspicion that witches weren't women who got kicked around by men, imprisoned in hopelessly dreary and self-denying domestic labor, and allowed no opinions, no adventures, no true existence of their own; and that is enough for her. She becomes one.[59]

Lesley's decision to convert is not based on the historical facts about modern Pagan witchcraft but on the strength of the fictional reality and the level of identification she shares with the character of the priestess portrayed in Bradley's opus. This is a powerful archetype, pioneered by Fortune but then disseminated to a whole new audience through *The Mists of Avalon*. Bradley's version of this motif is so popular that she is able to utilize her

---

58 Hutton, 355.
59 Ibid., 367.

success to promote other authors she favors through various editorial and collaborative projects.

Bradley's esoteric teachings and personal religious philosophies have been transmitted to a wider audience than that of her predecessor, due largely to the fact that they are presented solely as fiction and contain explicit references in this dialogue about women and power that reflect contemporary concerns. While her version of the priestess is inspired by Fortune's characters, her rendition is entirely unique. Her positioning of the priestess as working within a larger circle of peers and as an integral mediator of an active tradition are two of Bradley's innovations on this character, priestess type 3: Witch Queen.

Chapter 5

WITCH QUEEN

THE THREE WORKS to be analyzed in this chapter are Bradley's *The Mists of Avalon* (MA), *The Fall of Atlantis* (FA), and *The Firebrand* (FB). Presented as interpretations of seemingly unrelated mythologies, all three share a similarity of thematic elements and a corresponding development of the priestess character that lend themselves well to classification as a group and comparison with Fortune's trilogy of novels.

Each of these stories deals with themes of reincarnation as well as gender and religious identity. Each plotline centers around priestesses who are born to royalty and trained in an esoteric form of Goddess-centered religion and who struggle to maintain their religious and cultural traditions in the midst of a changing world and the rise of patriarchal religion. Despite the efforts of the protagonists, in each novel the established tradition is destroyed, but fragments of the old ways are preserved and grafted onto new beliefs. These rapidly fading traditions are presented as the final vestiges of the fictional *philosophia perennis* of the Dark Goddess that are reminiscent of Fortune's construction of Black Isis, the transcendental Great Goddess.

According to Paxson, the two most influential works on *The Mists of Avalon* are Fortune's *Sea Priestess* and *Moon Magic*. The obvious theoretical connections are the Atlantean mythology and esotericism that characterize Fortune's works, as well as the emphasis on the priestess as transmitter of the primordial cult of the Great Mother.

> And Morgan le Fay…had studied the symbols of cult after cult, for all worshipped the same things by different names and under different aspects, till at last she found that to which her own nature was attuned. And it was not the austere Egyptian faith, nor the radiant gods of Greece, but the primordial Brythonic cult that had its roots in Atlantis, which the dark Ionian Kelt shares with the Breton and the Basque.
>
> "For this," she said, "is older than the gods of the North, and there is more wisdom in it, for the gods of the North are mindless, being the formulations of fighting men; but the Great Goddess is older even than the gods that made the gods, for men knew the function of the mother before they understood the part played by the father…"[60]

The Fall of Atlantis is Bradley's interpretation of the Atlantean religion of the Great Mother that survives the destruction of the continent and spreads across the world. Previously titled *Web of Light/Web of Darkness*, by the end of the novel, the two sisters and priestesses Domaris and Deoris have been sworn to the service of the Dark Mother for all eternity, throughout all of their successive reincarnations. *The Mists of Avalon* details the dynastic end of a

---

60 Fortune, SP 127.

variant of the Atlantean Goddess religion that reached the British Isles. Using the framework of Arthurian legend, Bradley creates a college of priestesses dedicated to preserving the mysteries of the Great Mother at all costs that attempts to retain political power during the rise of patriarchal Christianity.

The sacred sisterhood is a core element of Bradley's fiction and integral to the concept of the priestess in her works. This circle of women, united through religion and often kinship, forms the basis of Bradley's idealized society. *The Firebrand* is based on the legend of the fall of Troy, the myth of *The Iliad* presented as a parable for the loss of Goddess-centered religions and the matrilinear line of descent. While this novel does not explicitly make reference to the Atlantean theory, it is included by virtue of its esoteric elements, college of priestesses devoted to the Dark Goddess, and parallel plot structure of indigenous matriarchal religions being replaced with patriarchal alternatives.

The character of the priestess is of central importance to all three works; the priestess's education and duties are similarly recurring themes. As many of the esoteric themes in Bradley's work utilize Fortune's theories, it is the character of the priestess that needs to be examined in order to differentiate each author's distinct voice.

Bradley's character Morgaine, despite her location in Arthurian myth, is the contemporary counterpart of the character first constructed in the works of Dion Fortune. Witch Queen is a related but distinct persona. As a new prototype, priestess type 3 embodies elements of the earlier, idealized modern priestess introduced by Fortune but differs as she incorporates themes of the woman warrior or female hero, as well as elements of feminine evil that Fortune avoids associating with her protagonists. The heroine only emerges in times of crisis, and not from Utopian situations; the heroine is a necessarily ambiguous figure that heralds a new order. The initial instability that creates the heroine is produced when consensus dissipates and expectations fail, and consequently, her actions are not always interpreted as heroic at the time. Villain and heroine are linked in that, depending on one's point of view, they can be the same woman. From the standpoint of the status quo, the innovators of a new religion are heretics. The ones outside of the accepted paradigm can easily be labeled lunatics or saints. It is only at the end of the quest, when the whole story is revealed, that it is possible to gauge success or failure.

Beset by such issues as abortion and religious doubt, Bradley's priestess is transformed from an idealized, omniscient stereotype into one that is fallible, with human flaws and weaknesses that make her accessible to the contemporary reader. In Bradley's works, the heroic priestess becomes the anti-hero, or one that has little control of outside events; often bewildered, deluded, ineffectual, and lost, the anti-hero is adrift in a world devoid of absolute values, yet she retains her dignity despite her defeats. Fortune's modern priestess, an embodiment of early feminist equality, becomes a postmodern icon in Bradley's construction of esoteric womanhood and demonstrates concerns of second-wave feminism of the twentieth century's latter half.

Priestess Type 3: Witch Queen

Priestess type 3, Witch Queen, combines many of the traits of her two predecessors, Earth Mother and Moon Mistress; however, she is not an everywoman character nor a simple amalgam of the two. Combining the charismatic personality and fertility of Earth Mother with the specialized training and advanced spiritualism of Moon Mistress, Witch Queen inherits all of the powers of her predecessors and wields a mighty, if fleeting, temporal political power as a result. All of the priestesses in Bradley's works are of royal descent, and in *The Mists of Avalon* (MA) and *The Fall of Atlantis* (FA), royal blood is a necessary prerequisite to becoming a full member of the priestess caste. While royal birth is not required for admittance to the different mystery religions that Kassandra is dedicated to in *The Firebrand* (FB), as a daughter of Priam, king of Troy, and Hecuba, queen of the royal line of the Amazonian tribe, she is both exposed to and accepted into two different and competitive traditions, that of the sun god Apollo and the Great Serpent, or Dark Mother.[61]

While this emphasis on lineage may seem antithetical to the archetypal priestess depicted in Fortune's novels, it is referred to extensively throughout the subtext of her works. Both examples of Earth Mother (before being paired off with affluent priests) are working-class women struggling to survive at the poverty level of the socioeconomic scale, and even Moon Mistress was originally a working girl in a theatrical troupe.[62] While the emphasis in Fortune's work is on the reincarnated soul, the subtext of

---

61   FB 87, 134–138, 230.
62   Fortune, SP 37.

the priestly Atlantean caste's sexual taboos and the reference to "the two Keltic stocks, the Breton and the Welsh"[63] of the Moon Mistress shows that race is also a recurring theme in Fortune's work. The blood matters; the powers of the priestess are, in part, derived from the right mixture of genetic material. Each race has its own psychic sensitivities and evolutionary goals. This concept of racial importance originated in H. P. Blavatsky's theories and has become a recurring theme in Western esoteric discourse ever since. This concept will be examined further in future chapters, but it is important to note here that the priestess is extremely concerned with the physical and spiritual evolution of her people.

The power of the Witch Queen relies heavily upon the king-making ritual referred to throughout *The Mists of Avalon* as the "Great Marriage."[64] This is a sexual rite involving a virgin priestess and the kingly candidate, intended to magically bind the king to the land; it is reminiscent of the sacrificial king of Frazer's *Golden Bough*.[65] This is another departure from Fortune's priestess archetype, who avoids physical sexual contact with her priests except for rare occasions. Unlike her predecessors, Witch Queen has certain sexual obligations that are incumbent with her title. She is required to bear a daughter in her service to the Goddess, as the royal blood of Avalon is passed matrilinearly; and, if selected, she must guard her virginity until the ruling Lady of Avalon decides it is time for her to lose it, usually in some magical pursuit.[66]

---

63 Ibid.
64 Bradley, *The Mists of Avalon*, 171.
65 Frazer, 7.
66 MA 16, 171.

Although the earlier Earth Mother of Fortune's works does have the option to marry her male counterpart—and, by implication, will eventually bear him children—this type of sexual compulsion and duty to bear children is not at all associated with either of Fortune's priestess models. However, this type of selective breeding is implied in the Atlantean subtext of both *Sea Priestess* and *Moon Magic*, and although it is not directly applied to the modern priestess, it is referred to as an ancient custom no longer kept.[67] Fortune's le Fay chooses to be celibate but is not commanded to do so. Fortune describes this shift away from the physical reenactment of religious ideals into an abstract or philosophical interaction as the result of astrological orientation:

> We are in the sign of Aquarius today. The workings are astral. That is why you get the ideal of celibacy in religious life instead of the old ideal of fecundity.[68]

Fortune's priestesses operate primarily through the astral manipulation of the energy of polarity, and for the most part do not describe literal or physical acts. Bradley's character is different. Witch Queen's astral magic manifests primarily as dreams and visions; the bulk of her magical rituals and mystical experience are connected with sex and/or childbirth.

Witch Queen has a duty to participate in the annual fertility rites of her queendom and a ritual role as the incarnation of the Goddess as Mother. This role is literal as well as symbolic in the

---

67 SP 108. "Very strictly did they guard the sacred blood, for it held the power of vision. But the priestesses were not married to any man, but mated with the priests as was required for magical purposes."

68 MM 136.

Avalonian custom of the Beltane fires, in which those faithful to the Goddess go out into the fields to bless the crops by having sex with their chosen companions. Within the context of the text, the participants are understood to be acting the part of Goddess and God, and children born of Beltane night are considered children of the gods.[69] This ritual is open to all of those who adhere to the Goddess religion and is not restricted to priestesses; however, unless they are given specific instructions to stay away from a higher-ranking superior, it is incumbent on the priestess to participate.

Although Bradley's Witch Queen advocates that choice of sexual partner, regardless of marital status, is a woman's Goddess-given right—and that institutional monogamy is blasphemous and an affront to the Goddess[70]—she does not advocate overt or promiscuous sexual behavior for women. The Witch Queen's preoccupation with physical sex is a significant departure from Fortune's priestess representation, which is usually characterized by a sublimation and redirection of sexual energy. The entirely sexual characterization of female power in *Mists* has drawn its strongest feminist critique as inherently phallocentric, yet masquerading under a matriarchal veneer. As Fuog states,

> The power of the women in *The Mists of Avalon* is inextricably linked to their sexuality. This linkage reinforces the patriarchal attitude that woman is a voracious and manipulative sexual creature.[71]

---

69 MA 153, 165.
70 FB 17 and MA 587.
71 Fuog, "Imprisoned in the Phallic Oak." This sentiment is echoed by James Noble, who states that "even in their sexual practices the

I do not dispute these claims but instead offer a corollary interpretation. Bradley's intent is to posit her reconstructionist history within a wider context of Western esotericism, which begins from a consensus of magical polarity, where there are distinct functions of positive and negative, male and female energies. The interaction of these forces is the energy that drives the universe, so sex is of fundamental importance to the construction of power in her presentation of women. Bradley is not writing as a feminist; she is writing as a practicing occultist, and this flavors the philosophy of her fiction. Each author who participates in this dialogue describes sex in a manner that promotes her esoteric worldview, which is based on the fundamental associations of women with the body, sexuality, and somatic experience that characterize Western thought. Therefore, in esoteric fiction sexuality is both the source of female power as well as female evil.

While this approach may seem regressive from a purely academic feminist standpoint, it is a theme that has a long history in occult philosophy and discourse, which has been greatly stimulated by the input of women. *The Mists of Avalon* introduced these ideas to a mainstream audience in a way that was radical not only for its inclusion of esoteric philosophy, but also for its inversion of established sexual taboo as a source of sacred power. Although such topics as homosexuality and occasional non-monogamy are embraced as healing, bonding acts, other taboos against promiscuity and prostitution are preserved. Presenting these themes

---

women of Avalon are merely imitating the predatory sexual rites of males in a patriarchal culture: the only difference is that it is men, as opposed to women, who become objectified for the purpose of satisfying sexual desire or engendering offspring" (Noble 150–151).

within the context of a society of women is one of the most powerful aspects of Bradley's collected works, of which Avalon's college of priestesses is the primary example. Whenever a society or caste is established, another class of outsiders necessarily arises. Although it has been argued that Bradley's representation of women in *Mists* reaffirms patriarchal attitudes, one could note that these portrayals of feminine evil actually make the concept of the priestess more believable by presenting a profane foil for the sacred ideal.

The recurring emphasis of motherhood as the primary symbol of femininity and spiritual authority, in addition to the importance of matrilinear succession, distinguishes other influences on Bradley's work outside of Dion Fortune, predominately those of feminist spirituality and Theosophical Catholicism. Bradley's Witch Queen resembles the construction of the World Mother popularized by the Theosophical Society in the 1920s and 1930s. Dixon describes this idealized conception of womanhood:

> As a priestess, the mother presided over the sacrament of birth... Motherhood was therefore a great initiation into spiritual mysteries, a transfiguration, an illumination, and an expansion of consciousness.[72]

As most of Witch Queen's power is derived from motherhood, with similar emphasis on all-female initiation rituals, this character is indicative of Bradley's varied interests and syncretic esoteric beliefs and is not a simple reworking of a previous motif.

Unlike Fortune, who never has more than one priestess at a time in each of her works, Bradley has a multitude of priestesses

---

72   Dixon, 214.

present at the same time in a text, usually as contemporaries of the others. Fortune's priestess is typically self-taught or guided by the moon; Bradley's priestesses are always formally trained by a group of elders and are the inheritors of an unbroken traditional initiatory lineage. This emphasis on the convent as opposed to the solitary woman is an interesting shift in how the priestess acquires her authority. In Fortune's works Everywoman is a reflection of the Goddess; with introspection and meditation upon the moon—and the help of a masculine counterpart—she is able to tap into the archetype at will. In Bradley's works the emphasis is on careful selection of candidates and formal training; all women may be representative of the Goddess, but not all women can become priestesses; they must be recognized as such by a circle of peers and undergo a series of initiations.[73] The power or authority of the priestess is thus passed from woman to woman, whereas in Fortune's works the initiation into the mystery is always cross-gendered.

This shift from a cross-gendered to a single-gendered focus is repeated throughout Bradley's fiction and has its roots in feminist spirituality. Almost all of the magical rituals in Bradley's texts, outside of certain exceptions such as the king-making ritual in *Mists*, involve women only; in Fortune's texts no magic is worked without a male priest to balance the polarity of the priestess. Bradley's texts often depict antagonism, if not outright hostility, between the priests and priestesses of the Goddess religion; in Fortune's works harmonious relationships between priestess and priest are a necessary prerequisite for magic to occur.

---

73 Bradley, *The Firebrand*, 138–139, FA 156–157, and MA 137.

The discrepancy is reflective of both authors' personal relationships and esoteric backgrounds. From the available data, it appears as if Fortune practiced magic primarily with men; Bradley's fiction features rituals developed after she had separated from her husband in 1979 amidst a close-knit circle of family and an all-female coven. Fortune's individual, idealized priestess is reinterpreted by Bradley as a participant in a mystical sisterhood of motherhood that functions almost entirely without men. While Fortune's fiction does include allusions to sexual segregation for the Atlantean priesthood, Bradley is the one who takes this idea to propose separate spiritual training for men and women, emphasizing the role of the priestess as the vital force of the Goddess religion.

Triple Goddess?

Another aspect of presenting a convent of priestesses, as opposed to portraying one at a time, is the ability to split the characteristics of the Goddess among them instead of containing all of the attributes of deity in one archetypal woman. This device allows Bradley to elaborate on the different aspects of the divine personality of the Goddess through the dispositions of a multiplicity of priestesses.

This unity of the Goddess characteristics among a diversity of characters is best summarized in the following passage:

> Viviane bent over and picked up the sleeping Morgaine in her arms, holding her with great tenderness.
> "She is not yet a maiden, and I not yet a wise-woman," she said, "but we are Three, Igraine. Together we make up the Goddess, and she is present here among us."

> Igraine wondered why she had not named their sister Morgause, and they were so open to one another that Viviane heard the words as if Igraine had spoken them aloud.
>
> She said in a whisper, and Igraine saw her shiver, "The Goddess has a fourth face, which is secret, and you should pray to her, as I do—as I do, Igraine—that Morgause will never wear that face."[74]

This contradictory portrait of the Goddess characterizes Bradley's work. Although the overt image of the Goddess follows the threefold, transcendental structure of Mother, Maiden, and Crone that characterizes most of feminist spirituality, this scene hints that there is an unknown, almost sinister side of the Goddess: a fourth face, one that is secret and shunned. Besides revealing the structure of the fourfold feminine Divine—Maiden, Mother, Wisewoman/Crone, Warrior/Dark Mother—this passage depicts the mixture of veneration and dread that the Witch Queen reserves for her Goddess, and the spectrum of divine attributes that Bradley's priestesses embody.

Unlike Earth Mother or Moon Mistress, who have an almost instant rapport with both Black and White aspects of their Isis, Witch Queen periodically avoids contact with the Dark Mother and, in fact, fears her.[75] The Warrior aspect of the Dark Mother takes on the militancy of the avenging angel, capable of cruelty as well as retribution, yet is an inescapable component to Bradley's construction of woman and priestess. This fourth aspect can be equated with Auerbach's feminine demonic with unknown powers of destruction. Each of these four aspects of Bradley's Goddess also corresponds with distinct stages in the life of a priestess. Morgaine comes to this realization at the end of *Mists*:

---

74 MA 23.
75 MA 96, FA 366–368, and FB 228.

> *I stood in the barge alone, and yet I knew there were others standing there with me, robed and crowned, Morgaine the Maiden, who had summoned Arthur to the running of the deer and the challenge of the King Stag, and Morgaine the Mother who had been torn asunder when Gwydion was born, and the Queen of North Wales, summoning the eclipse to send Accolon raging against Arthur, and the Dark Queen of Fairy...or was it the Death-crone who stood at my side?* [76]

The subtext of the Witch Queen suggests the angelic and demonic attributes of a fourfold Goddess rather than the overt explication of the transcendental Triple Goddess of feminist spirituality. Like Fortune's Black/White Isis, Bradley's Goddess is both creative and destructive, with dominion over life and death. However, Bradley's priestess, personified through the Witch Queen, also projects stereotypes of feminine evil and transmits the traditional fear of female sexuality to a contemporary audience. By presenting Morgause as a sexually promiscuous and ambitious foil to the priestess, and through the descriptions of sexual retribution that the women of Avalon enact upon their enemies, female sexuality is presented as a powerful tool for destruction.

Yet these negative elements are some of the most compelling aspects to the character of Witch Queen. She is complex and is both hero and villain at different parts in the tale, which makes the character accessible to a contemporary audience. She is flawed and acts as the anti-hero when her actions directly hinder or abate her spiritual progress. This concept is often tied in with the destruction or disbursement of the spiritual tradition that she is attempting to preserve. Witch Queen is often fatalistic and her story tragic, but her defeats are legendary. Her actions, whether

---

76   MA 867. Author's emphasis.

for good or ill, shine with a brilliant desperation against certain doom. The resilience of Witch Queen to persevere in the wake of personal tragedy and loss is one of the most poignant aspects of Bradley's depiction of the priestess.

Witch Queen can be considered half of a larger "Sacred Queen" motif that is explored throughout the Avalon series. Despite her obligation to pass along the sacred bloodline, she is similar to Moon Mistress in the sense that she is, for the most part, withdrawn from the outside world, focusing instead on spiritual matters, segregated from public life. While she works with males for specific rites, she remains unmarried and instead reserves her energy and resources for the training of new priestesses and maintenance of the Goddess religion.

Another take on the Sacred Queen theme is offered through the works of Diana L. Paxson and for the purposes of this book will be referred to as priestess type 4: Warrior Queen.

Chapter 6

DIANA L. PAXSON

DIANA L. PAXSON is a prolific author and active Pagan clergy. She was born in Detroit, Michigan, on February 20, 1943. An only child, her family relocated to Southern California when she was three years old. She attended Mills College in Oakland for her undergraduate work and eventually transferred to the University of California at Berkeley. She graduated in 1966 with a master's degree in comparative literature with a specialization in medieval literature. At this time, she decided to throw a medieval-themed party in her backyard that became the first tournament for what was later called the Society for Creative Anachronism, or SCA, on May 1, 1966. As was previously noted, Marion Zimmer Bradley is credited for naming the fledgling organization, but Paxson was the originator of the idea for the gathering, provided the space for the original event, and served on the board of directors for the first decade of its inception.

One of the original attendees of this event was her future husband, Don Studebaker (aka Jon DeCles) author, performer, and foster brother to Marion Zimmer Bradley. The two were wed in

DIANA L. PAXSON

1968 and moved into the communal home of Greyhaven. She had two sons and by 1976 had sold her first short stories. Throughout the 1970s Paxson began exploring Paganism and alternative religions, joining the Aquarian Order of the Restoration, a ceremonial group led by Marion Zimmer Bradley, based on the theories of Dion Fortune. In 1978, she and Bradley created Darkmoon Circle as an all-female group, mentioned previously as the inspiration for the college of priestesses in *Mists*. In 1982 she was consecrated as a Pagan priestess and her first novel was published in two parts, *Lady of Light* and *Lady of Darkness*.[77]

---

77 Information provided courtesy of personal communication with Diana L. Paxson.

Throughout the 1980s Paxson became an active leader in the Pagan community, establishing the Fellowship of the Spiral Path in 1986. She also served as first officer for Covenant of the Goddess in the early 1990s but became increasingly involved with Heathenism throughout this time, establishing Hrafnar Kindred in the late 1980s. This group practices Ásatrú, or Norse Paganism, and has a special focus on oracular and trance work, which has become the major focus of Paxson's nonfiction publications. In 1992 she joined the Troth, an international Heathen organization, and has since served as an elder and as a clergy trainer, as well as a variety of other roles. She is also the current editor of *Idunna*, the Troth's international journal. She has also been a regular contributor to the Sword and Sorceress series since its inception.

When Marion Zimmer Bradley's health began to decline in the mid 1990s, Paxson assisted in co-authoring several of the Avalon books and continued the series after Bradley's death in 1999. Throughout this time she has continued to participate in rituals and workshops at various Pagan festivals, and many of her works have been translated into German and other languages. She enjoys immense popularity worldwide and is an influential voice in contemporary Pagan discourse.

Recently she agreed to an interview discussing the construction of the priestess in her works and the Avalon series at large. We also discussed the role of Greyhaven in creating a writer's network, her personal experience as an author and priestess, and the direction that she has taken with the Avalon books.

SS: It is clear that the image of the priestess presented in the work of Dion Fortune is a direct influence on the characters in *The Mists of Avalon*. What would you say is one of the main differences between the priestesses of Bradley's works compared to Fortune's models?

DLP: Marion's priestesses follow a sequence of serving the Maiden, Mother, and Crone.

SS: A primary difference of note between the two authors' approaches are that Fortune always shows the priestess acting as a lone woman with a male partner, and Bradley's priestess is always the product of a college of peers or a sacred sisterhood.

DLP: True. The male partner completes the circuit of power so the magic can work. Marion's priestesses do the same kinds of rituals; for instance, in the Running of the Deer in *Mists*, in a setting which is like the one that Fortune refers to as having existed in ancient times.

SS: For the purposes of this study, I have focused primarily on your works in the Avalon series as a basis for our discussion of the character of the priestess. Is there a difference in the presentation of the priestess in the Avalon series from your solo work?

DLP: In the series I did my best to identify some of Marion's major perspectives and themes and build on them, but inevitably a lot of my own ideas came through. In some cases I was writing not what I thought Marion would have, but what she *should* have written. Looking at my solo work, especially *White Raven* and *Serpent's Tooth*, gives you an idea of where I started. For Marion's pre-*Mists* concepts you should also look at her Darkover books, especially *Thendara House* and *City of Sorcery*.

You also need to understand the writing process for the Avalon books. Marion was my sister-in-law and fellow priestess as well as a role model for being a female writer. She wrote *Mists of Avalon* during the first flourishing of feminist Wicca, when we were exploring women's spirituality and founding Darkmoon Circle. For all of us, understanding the role of a priestess was a major goal.

I had a master's degree in medieval literature and was able to loan her some books, as well as hold her hand while she worked on *Mists*. As she indicates in the foreword, the collegial spirit of Darkmoon Circle was part of her inspiration for the priestesses of Avalon. By the time she started *Forest House*, she had withdrawn from active participation in the Pagan community and had had several strokes. She finished a first draft, but it was unpublishable, so she handed it over to me. The basic plotline is based on the opera *Norma*, which, in typical nineteenth-century operatic fashion, ends with everyone dead. I suggested keeping Caillean alive to reactivate the college of priestesses on Avalon, thus connecting it to the Avalon series. This made everyone, especially the publishers, very happy.

They asked for another book. Realizing that Marion could only write short pieces by this time, I plotted *Lady of Avalon*. She wrote part of the beginning of part I and a little at the beginning of part III. The rest was my attempt to identify and explore her themes, including the mother/daughter relationship.

Priestess of Avalon was all my own idea and has a lot more actual history than Marion felt comfortable with, but it was my attempt to convey Marion's attitude toward religion and explain how she (as well as Dion Fortune) was able to simultaneously practice Paganism and Christianity. While I was working on this book I visited some friends in England who let me see some unpublished material on the Arthurian legend by Dion Fortune having to do with the roles of the king and the Lady of the Land. We all remarked on how close Marion, who had not seen this material, came in *Mists*.

Ancestors of Avalon is the sequel to Marion's *Fall of Atlantis*, which you should also consider in your analysis of priestess roles. *Atlantis* was originally written during the '50s. The difference between it and *Mists* shows the effect of feminism.

Although *Ravens of Avalon* is a direct prequel to *Forest House*, it is much more of a historical novel. I was trying to show how the community that we see in *Mists* might have evolved from a historical

Celtic practice plus the Avalonian tradition Marion invented.

In some ways, *Sword of Avalon* is the least connected to Marion's concepts, but rather draws more on my own concern with the role of the priestess in connection to the land, as well as a greater recognition of separate goddesses as distinct from the Great Goddess of feminist theology.

SS: I am really interested in finding out about your process when it comes to writing about the character of the priestess. You mention at the end of *Sword of Avalon* that there is an altar next to your desk that gives you inspiration, with items that are personally meaningful to you and symbolic to the work itself. Is this the usual way that you approach your writing? Is this specific to this series?

DLP: Since I myself am an active Pagan priestess, it is natural to involve the deities I am writing about in the process of creating a book that features them. The altar serves as a focus for contemplation and inspiration. Meditation allows the deities to speak to and through me. In *Ravens* I was so troubled by the tragedy of the Celtic defeat that I had to do a formal ritual to get the Morrigan's perspective.

SS: Kind of along those lines, were there any writing workshops or rituals that you participated in at Greyhaven or with Marion that are helpful when you write—anything that you would like to share with other aspiring female authors?

DLP: For many years, a lot of writers would gather at Greyhaven for Sunday afternoon tea, which inevitably featured a lot of discussion about writing. I also listened to Marion speak at many SF conventions. She had a very businesslike approach to writing, based more on solid technique and discipline than inspiration.

SS: How is it different to write within a community of like-minded individuals as opposed to writing alone? Can you describe the personal benefits and challenges of each approach that you have encountered?

DLP: My husband and brother-in-law were also writers, so living at Greyhaven was often like life in a writers' colony. We traded problems and encouragement, but in the end, the writing has to be done alone. From the spiritual point of view, the fact that my career as a writer and a priestess developed simultaneously meant that I was learning and practicing many of the same skills and rituals that I wrote about.

SS: Could you provide some biographical information, such as when you were married and when you decided to move into Greyhaven?

DLP: I married Donald Studebaker (better known as a writer and actor by the name Jon DeCles) on May 12, 1968. He became close to Marion's younger brother,

Paul Edwin Zimmer, when he was a teenager and lived with the family in upstate New York for several years before he, Paul, and Paul and Marion's mother came out to Berkeley in 1966 (just in time to help me found the Society for Creative Anachronism). At about the same time Paul got married, and since none of us had much money, Don and I and Paul and Tracy, along with Paul's (and Marion's) mother, all moved in together. Our first home was a rented house we called Rivendell. When the owner wanted her house back, we found Greyhaven, an estate sale fixer-upper, and through a series of miracles and loans from generous friends were able to make a down payment. By this time both Tracy and I had children, so we needed the space. This was just before housing prices began to rise, and pretty soon we were paying less on the mortgage for a fifteen-room house than most people were paying for apartments.

SS: In a previous interview you mentioned that the community at Greyhaven was an extended family unit based on the ideas presented in Heinlein's *Stranger in a Strange Land*. Could you elaborate on this description? How would you say that this alternative arrangement influenced your writing?

DLP: As things developed, it was more of an extended family than a Heinlein-style "nest." We were fortunate that Mom Zimmer was available to help with the children when the rest of us were working. Don and Paul were already serious about writing when we met in 1966. It took me until 1971 to get over the discouragement I suffered in a college creative writing class (they wanted us to write literary fiction, which I hated) and realize that real people (i.e., Marion) wrote books that real people (like my family) actually liked to read. At that point I started my first novel. Marion had been living in Berkeley when we started the SCA, but she moved East, so I didn't really get to know her until she and her family moved back to Berkeley. She very kindly read and critiqued my work, and eventually I produced something that would sell.

So, as I said earlier, living at Greyhaven was often like living in a writers' colony. Because we were all living together (and Marion was five minutes away), we were constantly encouraging and discussing what we were doing. When Don, Paul, and I were too obscure to get agents, we formed a family literary agency headed by Paul's wife, who was the only one of us who was not a writer. We all did market research, I wrote letters and mailed out manuscripts, and Tracy negotiated contracts. Eventually a couple of other local writers joined in. This was possible because in the '70s and '80s the science-fiction community was still small enough that most editors had once been fans and still came to SF cons, where authors could talk to them and sometimes persuade them to buy books.

SS: Was there a specific instance or experience in your past that first inspired you to investigate occult theory?

DLP: What I was looking for was not occult theory so much as spiritual experience. Since my mother had given me a goddess name, I read a lot of mythology. Like many others who ended up as Pagans, as a child I was "god hungry" and looked for inspiration in nature and old stories. I was so impressed by Dion Fortune's work because she made clear that the purpose of learning magic was not to gain power but to advance spiritually and to use esoteric knowledge to do good. "I seek to know in order that I may serve" is the initiate's vow.

SS: One of the most notable elements of your stories is an explicit discourse on the power of sex as a sacrament and healing force. When queen and king are united, the land flourishes; when they are apart, trouble such as war, spiritual distress, and natural disaster ensues. Fidelity is also a key concept in your fiction, but it seems to take on a different meaning than its typical equation with monogamy. Could you explain how these concepts of fidelity and sexual freedom influence the social code of the priestess?

DLP: The idea of king and queen as priest and priestess of the land comes from some of the interpretations of the Pagan and medieval past that became popular during the thirties (see authors like Naomi Mitchison and Margaret Murray, as well as Fraser's *Golden Bough*) and were carried into Wicca. Dion Fortune used some of these concepts in her novels and her interpretation of the Arthurian legend, and so did Marion in *Mists*.

In the old days, people took oaths for many things. The oath of monogamy in the Christian wedding service was only one of them. Even today, a soldier's oath to go risk his or her life may supersede his or her oath to take care of his or her family. In my opinion, the point is to choose your oaths carefully. Fidelity in marriage depends on what exactly you promised. That said, one advantage of monogamy is that balancing multiple commitments is hard. But sex is only one aspect of a marriage and not always the most important.

In the case of a king and queen who have taken oaths to their land and people, performing sexual magic to fulfill those oaths could easily take precedence over their personal relationship. And the sexual act is not necessarily what is needed. King and queen or priest and priestess can work with polarity and represent male and female energies in many other ways, as Le Fay does in *Moon Magic*. An unmarried priestess representing the Goddess can use her sexuality to serve the Goddess.

SS: What is the difference between a sorceress and a priestess? Is there a difference?

DLP: A priestess serves one or more gods and her community. She usually employs rituals and prayers but may or may not use magic. As the figure of the sorceress has developed, she uses magic for purposes that may or may not benefit others. She has magical abilities, which may come from power over spirits. A priestess (even of an evil god) is bound by some kind of code; a sorceress is bound only by her own will and the laws of magic. A priestess can also be a sorceress, but in general, the implication is that a priestess works with or for the Powers, whereas a sorceress makes them work for her.

SS: There seems to be a progression from your earlier fiction and short stories to your most recent publications. Obviously, these are all very different settings, different characters/concerns published over time, but is there a continuity to your image of the priestess? How would you characterize the evolution of the priestess in your works?

DLP: Wow, that's a hard one. In the Westria books the clergy remain unmarried, though they can have relationships, so that their first loyalty will be to the job. Priests or priestesses may be clergy attached to villages or households. Adepts, male or female, specialize in different kinds of magic and are independent. The magical system is based on polarity and the four elements. In *The White Raven* and *The Serpent's Tooth*, Branwen and Cordelia are queen-priestesses. In the Wodan's Children trilogy, Brunhild is essentially a priestess of Wodan. The Walkyriun are essentially witches who serve as village clergy, healers, etc. In the Avalon books I was developing the concept Marion created in *Mists of Avalon*, in which a group of priestesses (and priests) with special training work magic for the common good from Avalon or go out to serve the people. Which function should take precedence varies over the centuries.

I think that my concept of the work of a priestess depends first on the setting. If it is historical, or in an already established setting, I begin with what is known about the role in that time and place. However, I am sure that my concept has been shaped by my own work as a priestess during the past thirty years and the fact that I have been training Pagan clergy during most of that time.

SS: How have the works of Dion Fortune and Marion Zimmer Bradley affected your own work? How do the priestesses that you present coincide or diverge from the models that they present?

DLP: The literary fiction held up as a model when I was in college bored me. Realizing that a real person—Marion—wrote books that real people—me—really enjoyed reading was an epiphany, and I decided to reclaim my childhood ambition of writing. Marion believed that a story should have strong characters, a problem to solve, and a clear beginning, middle, and end. The stories she bought for Sword and Sorceress are examples of her taste, and the magazine gave a start to a number of successful women writers. When she published *The Fall of Atlantis*, I realized that it was possible to sell an adult book with esoteric content, which had not been the case a few years earlier.

Dion Fortune's novels were more relevant to me in my development as a priestess. I read everything, both fiction and nonfiction, that she had written, and it sometimes seemed to me that she was able to be more open about spiritual experience in fiction than she was in the nonfiction books. In a novel you can present the subjective experience of working magic. *Moon Magic* especially taught me a lot about what it was like to function as a priestess. However, as I indicate below, my career as a public priestess has been much more like that of Viviane or Anderle.

SS: The image of the Dark Mother is evocative and mysterious. While she is briefly mentioned in the works of Bradley (end of *Fall of Atlantis* and hinted at as a fourth face of the Goddess in *Mists*), you take this idea and give it further explication in your Avalon contributions. In *Sword of Avalon*, this side of the Goddess is the primary archetype that Anderle works with; as Lady of Avalon this is very far removed from Morgaine in *Mists*, who seems to fear the Dark Mother at times and seeks to avoid her in that form. Fortune's works emphasize a duality in the Goddess, White/Black Isis, and this seems to be echoed in the construction of Caratra/Ni-Terat you present in your works. Could you explain what the image of the Dark Mother means to you?

DLP: Hmm. I don't really think that Anderle works primarily with the Dark Mother. I do agree that the White/Black Isis and Caratra/Ni-Terat dichotomies are similar. The latter come from Marion's Atlantis mythos, which is the part of her work most directly inspired by Fortune. In *Mists*, Morgaine spends a lot of the book avoiding the Goddess in any form. The period in which she is most active as a priestess is actually not when she is at Avalon, but when she is Uriens' queen, when she is primarily a sorceress. To me, the Dark Mother is the recognition that power can be dangerous as well as beneficent, and that destruction is as natural and necessary a part of life as creation.

SS: One of the main themes that fascinates me is the power dynamic between the priestess with other women in her life. In *Sword of Avalon*, Tirilan has assumed a new role as Lady of the Land and utilizes her sexuality in a radical way instead of becoming the Lady of Avalon as her mother intended. Has she fulfilled the prophecy she received from the Hidden Queen that she would become a priestess, but not the type her mother would choose?

DLP: Starting with some of the comments on the subject in *Mists*, I concluded that over the centuries the community of Avalon alternates between retreating from the world and attempting to change it, as Viviane does with all her machinations in *Mists*. Not too surprisingly, the best plots come from periods in which Avalon is taking action. A related repeating pattern is the conflict between tradition and innovation. Innovation often occurs in response to historical change. This is a somewhat different perspective on the Anderle/Tirilan relationship than the one you offer above.

SS: Could you describe this new type of priestess? How is she connected to the previous renditions of the priestess in the works of Fortune and Bradley? This study has focused primarily on the historical origins of the priestess in literature; where do you see it heading into the future?

DLP: I think that this is one of the points at which I was developing the concept in a direction that is not really implicit in what Marion had done. As Lady of the Land, Tirilan is not a camp follower but the High King's equal. With a worthy king Anderle could have played this role, but instead her greatest contribution is to act as priestess of the forge goddess so that Velantos can create the sword. Her contribution is to preserve the old ways of Avalon long enough to serve as a foundation for something new.

The difference in scale between Dion Fortune's novel and the Avalon books makes comparison difficult. Fortune's priestesses are like Caillean at the beginning of *Lady of Avalon*, trying to gather the remnants of a suppressed knowledge, reactivate the tradition, and reconnect with the power. Fortune's books are too short to do more than focus on a personal perspective. A greater tradition is implied but only revealed in flashes. Fortune's priestesses work independently, guided by nonphysical powers, rather than in the context of a spiritual community, even though Fortune herself had a community and was drawing on the traditions of the Order of the Golden Dawn. Her priestesses work magic in secret to change the spiritual currents that shape society. Her model is the solo magician or, at most, the magical lodge. By the '80s, the Pagan revival was becoming a vigorous public community, and the college of priestesses on Avalon, although it also works esoterically, is visible in the world, and priestesses were becoming clergy.

Marion and I were consecrated as priestesses together in 1982. Since then I have founded and/or led several Pagan organizations of various sizes, as well as training Pagan clergy. My perspective is therefore very much that of a priestess in a living tradition that is active in the world. Both Anderle and Tirilan act as leaders in their society. Anderle is the guardian of an esoteric tradition. Tirilan, however, is even more engaged with the outside world, and at a time when the major challenge to her land is climate change, she needs to connect the king to the land. This is certainly one of the roles that priestesses seem to have taken historically. Leadership in environmental protection is an area in which Pagans of all kinds are active.

My own perspective has also been evolving from a focus on divine archetypes to specific deities. The Avalonian mythos is firmly based on the concept of the Great Goddess and the Triple Goddess—Maiden/Mother/Crone—and that has to be retained; however, you will notice that in the more recent books, there is more emphasis on specific goddesses such as the Morrigan and the Lady of the Forge.

SS: What does the image of the sword symbolize to you?

DLP: In the Arthurian context, the sword comes from the Goddess and is given to the king as an emblem and channel of power. Symbolically, the relationship is probably similar to that between the Hindu gods and their consorts—they are so often shown embraced because it is the Goddess who activates the power of the God. For Mikantor, and later Arthur, receiving the sword demonstrates that the Goddess has empowered him to rule. I tried to show this relationship in the sword-forging scene in which Velantos does all the work, but the forge goddess, through Anderle, gives him the knowledge and power to do it. A sword is a tool to defend, to deal death, or to cut away what needs to be destroyed.

Chapter 7

WARRIOR QUEEN

THE FINAL CHARACTERIZATION of the priestess motif to be analyzed is priestess type 4: Warrior Queen. This is a term that is used to demarcate a specific kind of priestess that Paxson introduces to the Avalon series and is to be understood as a separate interpretation of the Sacred Queen motif first introduced by Bradley in *The Mists of Avalon*.

The works that will be reviewed for this character are *Ancestors of Avalon* (AA), *Ravens of Avalon* (RA), and *Sword of Avalon* (SA). These works were selected as independent contributions of Paxson to the series, which include theories that can be found in Paxson's other novels. It is important to keep in mind that although they are Paxson's original work, they are written to fit within the Avalon framework developed by Bradley. This distinction is necessary to understand how the Warrior Queen is connected to previous renditions of the priestess motif and also how she differs by incorporating the unique esoteric concerns of her creator.

It is appropriate here to review the terminology used in this book. The terms Earth Mother, Moon Mistress, Witch Queen, and Warrior Queen are intended solely to be used to demarcate distinct forms of the fictional priestess. They are provided as a convenient means to define separate forms of this motif within the parameters of this discussion, and they lose coherence when taken out of this context. The authors examined in this study have produced numerous works, both fiction and nonfiction, and these terms are not meant to be applied as blanket generalizations to the bulk of their esoteric thought. They are used simply to examine a small segment of the authors' concepts within a fictional framework and to inspire further interest in the topic of female identity within an esoteric context.

Priestess Type 4: Warrior Queen

As her name suggests, Warrior Queen deals primarily in blood. She is typically connected to a royal house, such as the royal blood of Avalon, and is charged with the maintenance and preservation of her tribe. Unlike previous models of the priestess, Warrior Queen conveys many traditional conceptions of womanhood. As a member of the ruling house, she is often concerned with the daily details of running a large household and educating the children, as well as making political decisions that affect her subjects. She is the mother of her tribe, the physical vessel of Goddess, the sacred and secular leader as Lady of the Land. She grants sovereignty to the king as a result of his pact with the land, which is incorporated into their wedding vows and blessed by their union. When queen and king are at odds or separated, there is peril in the land; when united, the tribe prospers.

However, as her story is often framed within a larger context of crisis, whether it be war, political turmoil, or environmental disaster, her attempts to uphold the traditions of her people are often eclipsed by the challenge of mere survival. Beset by these difficulties, Warrior Queen is often put in the position of having to fight for her life and for those in her care, and consequently she abandons elements of her training or early philosophies that do not serve her in these goals. She has a sacred duty to preserve the traditions and beliefs of her tribe but is often opposed by the circumstances of her dynamic environment. As a result, Warrior Queen is a pragmatist, progressive in her spiritual and political beliefs. She is a fighter, but her conflicts are not always physical, so she uses her many talents to reach diplomatic solutions.

While she is raised in the same tradition as Witch Queen and serves as part of the sacred sisterhood of Avalon, there are several key differences between these two interpretations of the Sacred Queen. While Witch Queen captures the formality of Fortune's Moon Mistress, Warrior Queen displays the nurturing qualities of Earth Mother. Warrior Queen is always paired with a male counterpart, and this pairing is a necessary step in accessing her potential and full power. Tiriki and Micail are featured in *Ancestors of Avalon*, Boudica and Prasutagos in *Ravens of Avalon*, and two couples in *Sword of Avalon*, Anderle/Velantos and the younger Tirilan and Mikantor. Warrior Queen's magic is usually cross-gendered, whereas Witch Queen works primarily with women, with men joining in ritual only for special occasions.

All versions of the Sacred Queen participate in the Great Marriage, uniting a chosen hero with the land. However, depending on the proximity of her partner, Warrior Queen has the opportunity to use the power raised by this rite in different ways. When sex is used to make political alliances, the power is used to bless the participants and the land. When sex is used to consecrate rituals or artifacts, as in the creation of Excalibur in *Sword of Avalon*, the energy raised charges the rite or object with a specific intent. Another aspect of Paxson's alternative approach to the Avalon mythos is to include an emphasis on the initiatory journey of the men in her stories as a separate but complementary series of events that is integral to the establishment and history of Avalon. One example of this new emphasis is on the communal education of both men and women together, which differs from Bradley's model of sex-segregated training.

This inclusion of men as central protagonists and working partners of the Warrior Queen greatly differs from the interactions of Bradley's characters but is reminiscent of Fortune's priestesses. Witch Queen is primarily concerned with the preservation of the female-oriented traditions of Avalon and is often removed from the world in spiritual seclusion. Warrior Queen does not spend the majority of her time cloistered within the sacred sisterhood but instead is active in the outside world as a political figure. She is often working alongside her man, or, if separated, working toward common goals. Warrior Queen is both a midwife to the newborn and a spiritual guide for the dead. She is connected to the land through the Great Marriage; by consummating the ritual, she is bound to both the king and the land. Marriage, whether legal or esoteric, is of central importance to Paxson's work.

Warrior Queen's function is similar to Earth Mother because she serves as the vital link between humankind, the land, and the gods. She differs from Earth Mother in that she is focused on the preservation of the tribe through child-bearing and education, in addition to her spiritual obligations. By her own admission, Fortune's depiction of Earth Mother is not necessarily the breeding type. While Witch Queen does bear children to the priestly caste in order to preserve the bloodline and psychic gifts of her tribe, she is not directly responsible for their care. Witch Queen emerges from a dedicated commune of women who share the domestic responsibilities, and the children are raised by the community at large. Warrior Queen usually comes from a complicated web of family and friends, has a closer relationship with her children, and is responsible for their primary care. This could be due, in part, to the fact that Warrior Queen typically begins having children at a much later age than Witch Queen. Despite her location in the mythical past, Warrior Queen is presented as at least being eighteen years old before entering marriage or bearing children, while Witch Queen becomes sexually active after menarche.

In *Ancestors of Avalon*, Tiriki and Micail are sent out to fulfill the prophecy that they will establish a new temple to replace the lost religion of Atlantis. Early on in the novel they become separated, and both attempt to fulfill the prophecy on their own for five years before being reunited. The environmental catastrophe that has led to their flight from their homeland is amplified by the fact that the survivors are forced to deal with a climate alien to the one that they have always known, and much of Tiriki's efforts are focused on connecting with the spirit of the new land and working out an effective survival strategy for her people. Throughout the course of the story, much of the old ways of Atlantis are lost or abandoned by Tiriki's group in favor of adapting new techniques and integrating with the native cultures of the island. Tiriki discovers that the Mysteries of the Mother are present on the new island and visits the wisewoman of the marshfolk, Taret, who recognizes her as a priestess of the Great Mother and offers initiation into their Mysteries. Tiriki concludes that perhaps her true mission is to create a completely new religion that includes native beliefs, rather than merely to exclusively preserve the high magic of Atlantis.[78]

Micail's group focuses primarily on reconstructing the old way of Atlantis, complete with the caste system in addition to constructing magical weapons, an effort that is eventually abandoned as several characters are killed in the process. He comes ashore amidst an Atlantean colony that has been established for at least a year, with its own offshoot of the Blue Temple, dedicated to Caratra instead of Ni-Terat. This is not the only change for the followers of the Goddess religion of Atlantis. The following passage describes this new representation of the Goddess:

> On the eastern wall the Goddess was pictured as a maiden dancing among flowers. The southern wall bore a mural of Caratra as Mother, enthroned with a laughing child upon her knee and all the fruits of the earth around her. In the west was the familiar representation of Ni-Terat, veiled with grey mystery, crowned with stars; but the north wall set Elara's heart to pounding, for there the Goddess was shown standing with a sword in hand, and her face was a skull.[79]

This fourfold representation of the Goddess is presented as an initiatory secret of the priestesses and is separate from the familiar triple form that is known to most women in the story. This is an interesting development in the Goddess theology of Avalon,

---

78 Paxson, *Marion Zimmer Bradley's Ancestors of Avalon*, 113.
79 Ibid., 137.

as this is the first time that a fourfold Divine is overtly acknowledged in the series. As this is the novel meant to connect Bradley's *Fall of Atlantis* with Avalon, this story recounts the beginnings of several themes in the series. Tiriki's daughter is the beginning of the royal bloodline of Avalon, the Tor is established as the center of the new temple, and the tithe of the marshfolk to support the clergy of Avalon is also initiated. While much of the caste structure of Atlantis is no longer applicable in the new land, the plotline suggests that there are enough survivors reared in these ways to establish an offshoot of this social code in the new land.

Ravens of Avalon takes place many centuries later, approximately 43–60 CE. This story centers around Boudica, a Celtic princess who is sent to study with the Druids on the Isle of Mona. She is sent to Avalon to participate in a puberty ritual and decide whether or not to become a priestess. Boudica chooses to return to her land and marry, but forges a close connection with Lhiannon, the priestess whom she has favored throughout her training. While in Mona, Boudica is possessed by the Morrigan, a battle goddess who prophesies the inevitability of the Roman invasion that the priestesses of Avalon are trying to circumvent.[80] This event marks the beginning of Boudica's work in the world, for her father has decided to submit to the Romans and swears his tribe to their authority. Although she is a Warrior Queen, she strives to maintain peace between the native Britons and the invading Romans by becoming a vassal to the Empire. She marries Prasutagos to cement political alliance between the Iceni tribes but disappears after the ceremony is performed, riding into the countryside for her husband to come

---

80 Paxson, *Marion Zimmer Bradley's The Ravens of Avalon*, 76–78.

and fetch her. They are united after a few days and return to his home to manage their lands under Roman rule.

Meanwhile, Lhiannon is visiting tribes that are resisting Roman rule, and she uses her magic to defend them and support the uprising. Even though Lhiannon is a priestess who fights, she is not a Warrior Queen. She chooses to remain a virgin, and therefore does not make the pledge with her body to unite the hero with the land; her potential mate in the text takes another wife, so she remains alone. Paxson attaches special status to virginity in this text, stating that it confers special oracular powers. This is the first time that continued virginity is presented as an option for the priestess in the Avalon model. For the most part, Lhiannon does more active fighting than Boudica throughout most of the text, intent on preserving Briton independence and the Avalon tradition. Lhiannon is often involved with the internal politics of the Priestesshood, in addition to influencing the exterior politics of the rebellion.

Boudica's story depicts the struggles of maintaining everyday life in the midst of civil chaos as she deals with the premature birth and death of her first child, political turmoil, and marital strife with her husband. During this time, the Romans succeed in disarming the populace and proceed to kill those who oppose the confiscation of their weapons. This act effectively wipes out a significant segment of the local males. Prasutagos becomes the sole candidate left to be named High King over the remaining Iceni tribes. Boudica agrees to participate in the king-making ritual in the traditional way, and the marriage is consummated anew.

This leads to a period of domestic ease for Boudica, juxtaposed with constant fighting for Lhiannon, who is finally ordered by the ruling Lady of Avalon to escape the destruction of Avalon and to preserve its traditions. Meanwhile, the Roman occupation continues to demand more tribute from the British vassals. Caratac, the British defender of the land, is betrayed and sent to Rome in chains, and Prasutagos dies. Boudica's last pledge to him is to defend their daughters and their land.[81] The remaining Iceni elect to name Boudica as their ruler until her daughters come of age to marry, and she assents to honor Prasutagos's last wish.

Boudica is bound to the land in an entirely new and different way than any of her predecessors. She makes a blood oath to guard the people of the Iceni as Lady of the Land, to act as its defender, and she swears by a collection of gods and goddesses, as well as her ancestors, that if she fails in this capacity, "may the sky fall and cover me, may the earth give way beneath me, and may the waters swallow my bones."[82] This passage demonstrates another key difference of Warrior Queen, who acts as a direct conduit of the spirit of the land and offers herself as the sacrifice if the king is incapacitated. She takes up arms when her home or clan are threatened instead of naming a masculine champion to fight for her.

The death of Prasutagos shatters the Iceni peace with Rome. Boudica is publically humiliated and whipped in front of her subjects, and her daughters are raped by soldiers. The goddess Cathubodva, also called the Morrigan, takes over Boudica's body and breaks through her restraints, killing the Romans who attacked the royal women. Boudica makes a pact with the

---

81   Ibid., 269.
82   Ibid., 282.

Morrigan to lead the people into a final act of rebellion against the invaders. Similarly, the remaining Druids also invoke the Morrigan to drive the Romans from their shores. The countryside erupts in chaos, and the Druid stronghold at Mona is finally breached. Lhiannon is spared, but Romans rape the women of the shrine and kill whatever men they find.[83]

On the eve of battle, Boudica is granted a strange vision of herself weeping and beating laundry, and this image advises the queen to abandon the cause—that she will not survive if she enters the battlefield. Boudica accuses the woman of being the Goddess in disguise, the real power that has led the people to this fight. The figure disagrees, and the following passage ensues:

> The woman shook her head. "They would say they followed Boudica."
>
> "But You are the one with the power!"
>
> "My heart is your heart. My rage is your rage. You are the Goddess—"
>
> Boudica realized that as the woman spoke she was saying the words as well. She shook her head in desperation. Was this a delusion, or has she been deluding herself all along?
>
> "And are my hands Your hands?" she cried.
>
> The woman got to her feet and Boudica saw herself reflected in the Other's eyes.
>
> "Only when you allow Me to use them," came the soft reply. "You shape the gods as We shape you. But the forms in which you see Us have been honed through many lives of men. Through Us you pass from mortality to eternity. Through Us, the Divine becomes manifest in you."[84]

---

83 Ibid., 320.
84 Ibid., 359.

After the battle, Lhiannon takes the severely wounded Boudica back to Avalon. There they call upon the Morrigan a final time for counsel, and she demands that Boudica be sacrificed in order to return peace to the land. In a startling scene, her veins are ritualistically opened up and her body is submerged in the sacred pool so that her blood can flow into the Holy Well and bless the land.[85] The novel concludes with an image of the Goddess accepting the sacrifice with the God beside her, who are presented as extensions of Boudica and Prasutagos, united in death once more.

THE LAST BOOK to be reviewed in this section is *Sword of Avalon*, set roughly in the time period of 1200 BCE at the end of the Bronze Age. This is the story of the creation of the sword Excalibur featured in the Arthurian myth. While the familiar trope of the Warrior Queen and consort is utilized, there is also another version of the cooperation/conflict model of connected priestesses demonstrated by the relationship of Anderle and her daughter, Tirilan.

Anderle, as Lady of Avalon, is intent on preserving the customs and passing on the seat of power to her daughter and heir. Tirilan is not interested in following in her mother's footsteps and instead wishes to become wife to Mikantor. This dissent between the women demonstrates different interpretations of what it means to be a priestess, with Anderle representing the tradition and Tirilan representing a new perspective.

---

85 Ibid., 389.

While pregnant with Tirilan, Anderle saves her infant nephew and heir to the throne, Mikantor, from being killed by traitors; they flee while his home is razed. In order to get cover from their followers, Anderle invokes the ancestors of the boy, who come to their aid.[86] This type of ancestor worship is unique to Paxson's characters in the series and is explicated in great detail through several rituals in her novels. It is worth noting because this is another example of the evolution of the duties of the priestess, who not only has an obligation to the preservation of the spiritual education of the living but also a commitment to honor the deceased with offerings and specific rites. This behavior allows the Warrior Queen to call upon the ancestors for help and guidance in times of great peril and distress.

They escape, and Tirilan is raised to take Anderle's place as Lady of Avalon while Mikantor is fostered among the marshfolk in secret. He eventually comes to Avalon as part of a new program created by the sacred sisterhood in which males and females are fostered on Avalon to be educated and make connections that will hopefully discourage the constant warring of the tribes. As the children grow closer, Tirilan confides to her mother that she will marry the boy one day.

Anderle is not pleased and informs her daughter that this is impossible. "You may take him as your lover in the rites, but priestesses do not marry."[87] Tirilan states that she wants a different life than the one that Anderle has chosen for her, and this

---

86 Paxson, *Marion Zimmer Bradley's Sword of Avalon*, 17.
87 Ibid., 78.

scene is the first conflict between mother and daughter regarding the expected duties of the priestess to her caste and tribe.

Mikantor's enemies discover that he is still alive; despite all of the care that has been taken to disguise his identity, he is captured. His captors decide to sell him as a slave, and he is sent overseas to a new land. This begins his initiatory journey in which he is taught the ways of war and is apprenticed to the blacksmith Velantos. Like *Ancestors*, this plot incorporates the actions of the male protagonists, and the fate of the land is similarly tied to the hero assuming his destined role as champion. As the story of Mikantor's exile unfolds, civil unrest and severe weather cause distress amongst the tribes on the Island of the Mighty. Through similar calamities, Mikantor returns home with Velentos to claim his destiny as defender of the land.

Tirilan takes the vows of a priestess, though she does so without joy, since she believes that Mikantor is dead. She swears to pledge her body to the service of the Goddess and to only have sex at the appointed times of ritual requirement.[88] However, at the time of her ritual ordeal, she is granted a vision of the Hidden Queen, who tells her that she will not be the priestess that her mother would make her—instead, her destiny lies with supporting the lord of the land. Tirilan returns to Avalon to confront her mother, furious to learn that Anderle suspected he had survived, and learns that Mikantor is on the way. The smith and the champion arrive at Avalon to receive the blessing of Anderle, train men to stand against the false king Galid, and forge new weapons.

---

88 Ibid., 211.

It is decided that to unite all the tribes of the island, Mikantor must perform the Running of the Deer ritual, or Great Rite, with a chosen virgin. Anderle demarcates Tirilan for the role, assuming that she will give up her claim on him once the rite is finished. This plan backfires, as Tirilan decides to leave Avalon and follow Mikantor on his quest to rid the land of the tyrant. Despite her mother's objections, she turns aside from the regular path of the priestess to become a Warrior Queen, to care for and assist her mate as he fulfills his destiny. This is a revolutionary act on her part, completely defiant of her training and upbringing. However, her adherence to the customs of Avalon keep her from revealing her full relationship with Mikantor, so her status is nebulous throughout much of the text. At the annual gathering of the tribes, Tirilan is finally acknowledged as Mikantor's lady and agrees to be the go-between for the queens of the tribes and the defender.[89] This recognition separates the pair; like the Warrior Queens in the previous texts, Tirilan must go on alone to bind the queens of the land to the cause as Mikantor goes to find men to help him defeat Galid.

Tirilan begins her task of learning the various Mysteries of the tribes and is taken hostage by Galid. Although he threatens her with violence and rape, he decides to lock her away instead, keeping her in the dark on starvation rations. She falls back on the disciplines of Avalon and spends most of her time in trance. When Galid returns he threatens her again, and Tirilan uses nonviolence as a weapon against him. She offers her blood and her body to

---

89 Paxson, *Marion Zimmer Bradley's Sword of Avalon*, 335.

him peacefully on the condition that he desists making war.[90] He refuses, and she is left to rot in her cell. Meanwhile, Velantos and Anderle perform a ritual to invoke the Lady of the Forge, a goddess that Velantos honors in his work as a smith, to instruct them on how to forge the sword, and proceed to channel their sexual desire into the rite. For three days they work on the blade, and when it is completed they consummate its creation with sex.[91]

Immediately upon its completion, Anderle flees to save Tirilan, and Velantos takes the sword in pursuit of them both to Azan, where Mikantor is racing to challenge Galid. The smith is taken and Galid confiscates the sword, then stabs Velentos with it. The smith manages to get away, and Mikantor draws the sword from Velentos to kill Galid.[92] After the battle it is decided to sheathe the sword in times of peace, and Tirilan is given the sword for safekeeping. Mikantor swears fealty to her, and she is given the authority to say when it shall be used again. The vision of her initiatory ordeal has been realized; she is a new kind of priestess, the Lady of the Land.[93] This ending also sets up the concept explored in *The Mists of Avalon* wherein the priestesses are the keepers of Excalibur and are the ones to name the time and the man who will wield it.

E Pluribus Unum

Paxson's Avalon novels feature a personal connection of her priestesses with local or tribal deities rather than an emphasis on

---

90 Ibid., 357.
91 Ibid., 360–373.
92 Ibid., 415.
93 Ibid., 419.

the transcendental figure of the Great Goddess of earlier authors. This representation is always countered with a philosophical discussion of the nature of the Goddess, typically presented within an educational setting of youngsters having theology lessons. The phrase "all gods are one, and there is only one initiator" is directly influenced by the ideas of Dion Fortune and appears frequently in the Paxson texts in one form or another. Paxson moves away from the characterization of the Triple Goddess that is emphasized in Bradley's work and instead incorporates various mythologies into her stories. After the concept of a multiplicity of deities reflecting one ideal is established, her stories tend to focus on the one particular facet, or face, of the Goddess that is intimately connected to the female protagonist and the particular plot of land that is the setting of the story.

For Tiriki in *Ancestors of Avalon*, her main focus is to survive in a foreign land. Synchronizing her own energies with her new home reveals that she must develop a greater understanding of the Dark Mother and learn the face of the Goddess in the new land rather than try to merely replicate the solar Atlantean religion. Boudica in *Ravens of Avalon* is clearly the chosen vessel of the Morrigan and is possessed by the goddess on more than one occasion, with or without her consent. However, in her role as queen of the tribe, she also works with the totem of her people, one being the White Mare and a regional deity.

In *Sword of Avalon*, Anderle works with several goddesses, though the one she most frequently mentions in the text is Ni-Terat, the Dark Mother. However, when she assists in forging the sword, it is the Lady of the Forge who is invoked and speaks through Anderle to help the smith complete the work. Tirilan has an alternate path and attempts to become the symbol of the Mother to all of the tribes she is trying to unite under Mikantor's banner, so she learns how to connect with the goddess that each tribe reveres, which is different depending on the location.

This emphasis on the personal nature of the Goddess is a hallmark of Paxson's work and is not limited to the Avalon series. However, its introduction into the Avalon mythos is intriguing because it brings a new interpretation to the Goddess religion that is entirely dependent on the region as well as the priestess's personality in the story. Paxson does not reject the idea of an abstract, transcendental Female Divine that characterizes previous works, but her focus is primarily on the independent, personal relationship of each priestess to her goddess. This is evidenced by the conversational dialogue between the priestess and goddess, which characterizes much of Paxson's work and is entirely absent from the work of Bradley and Fortune. In fact, the line between priestess and Goddess becomes increasingly blurred, with all of the Warrior Queens having doubts as to whether the Goddess is a separate entity at all or just another facet of their own personalities. This concept is reinforced by visions of the deceased characters as reflections of the gods, a device that is used in the conclusions of both RA and SA.

This subjective interpretation of the Goddess is reflective of the time in which Warrior Queen has been created, not the time in which the story takes place. For all that she is placed within historical and prehistorical settings, Warrior Queen is a postmodern construct as she reflects many of the contemporary concerns of the latter twentieth century. Environmentalism, birth control, religious pluralism, and religious doubt are all recurring themes in her story, and the image of the Goddess that is favored by each Warrior Queen is similarly influenced by these concerns. Is the Goddess a separate transcendental being or is she a personal extension of the self, a direct reflection of the aspirations and fears of the people who serve her? In Paxson's novels the answer to this question appears to be both. The concept of the Triple Goddess is retained as the transcendental ideal of the fertility cycle of most women, and the fourth face of the Goddess is the personal deity who guides the priestess, offering counsel or admonishment, or even the priestess herself. The fourth aspect can also be terrifying and violent. This face is also presented as an extension of her own consciousness, so it is unclear as to whether messages received from this source are indeed guidance from the Divine or merely wish fulfillment on the part of the character.

This is a problem, because the priestess in the novel still has to make decisions that affect the lives of those around her, regardless of any message from the Divine. In times of spiritual crisis, she often falls back on her early training for guidance and ethical clarity. So what does this training indicate is the appropriate behavior of the priestess? Which actions are sanctioned, and which are taboo? Who falls outside of this paradigm?

The next chapter presents the problem of feminine evil in a society that worships a female ideal and how these concepts have changed from one author to the next.

Chapter 8

THE PRIESTESS AND THE PROBLEM OF FEMININE EVIL

IN ALL OF the selected works, the priestess plays an intimate role in the physical well-being and spiritual development of her culture. As a product of occultism and women's spirituality, the fictional priestess uses magic and esoteric theory that is based on early twentieth-century scientific and religious imagination in an effort to accomplish these tasks. Eugenics, biological determinism, and female sexuality are combined to produce a worldview that is radically modern yet presented as a primordial tradition of Goddess worship. This chapter explores how the character of the priestess embodies and promotes these ideas for a contemporary audience.

The Magic of Biological Determinism

One recurrent image that serves as the ultimate symbol of female perversity, which haunted the Victorian mind, is that of the priestess with the severed head. The image of Salome, in vogue at the end of the nineteenth century in both literature and art, represents all the themes of racial and evolutionary degeneracy associated with women at the time. Salome, as the epitome of the female predator, became a repository for all of the antifeminist thought and the personification of emasculating feminine evil. Like the image of Circe that also proliferated in turn of the century art and literature, Salome embodies the destructive sexual power traditionally attributed to women.[94] In order to reconstruct female identity, women in the early twentieth century had to overcome these stereotypes by first accepting these images as part of the standard dialogue, then supplying their own meanings.

In order to disassociate the modern priestess from the negative connotations of her representation as Salome, symbol of female aggression and racial degeneracy, Dion Fortune associates her characters with the cutting edge of the occult and scientific theory of her time: the idea of gendered biology that continues to dominate the majority of scientific thought today. Biological determinism assumes a sexually dimorphic universe in which there is an opposite but complementary function of male and female gender, assigning stereotypic attributes and behaviors (such as aggressiveness to males and passivity to females) to all types of living organisms.

This paradigm of binary gender often presupposes male supremacy by superimposing cultural norms onto biological terms, often through culturally distorted language (such as using the term *harem* to denote a group of females with a single male). As a result, the male is the example of the normative sex, and the female is a deviation from the ideal. This model of science

---

94 Dijkstra, *Idols of Perversity*, 385–400.

leads to social speculation as generalization leads to universalization and "natural laws" are used to uphold societal and religious norms that often include racist or classist conceptions of the human condition. Contemporary theory attempts to include new viewpoints, yet much of the current conversation begins with these basic hierarchal assumptions that infuse classical Western thought.

This theory of biological determinism, a foundation of Western science, also permeates Western Esotericism, and is prevalent in the works of female authors from Blavatsky to the present day. While concepts such as racism and classism were endemic to Western culture prior to the works of Helena P. Blavatsky, she was the first to exonerate and codify these beliefs by providing a spiritual justification for their inclusion in modern scientific theory. Blavatsky's racial conception of spirituality was widely accepted in the West in no small part because it capitalized on the popular theories of biological determinism and sexual dimorphism that dominated the standard narrative of the times. Despite the repugnance of these ideas to the contemporary mind, the inclusion of these concepts allowed Blavatsky to introduce her radical message of magic being the missing link between science and religion. At the end of the nineteenth century, ideas such as sexual equality and female empowerment outside of marriage were only feasible when paired with the familiar concepts of elitism and racism. This proved to be an extremely marketable philosophy, as evidenced by Helena P. Blavatsky's subsequent meteoric success.

Women around the world may have embraced many of these ideas because the concept of motherhood, whether spiritual or physical, is intricately connected to concepts of cultural identity.

Women are the physical bridge from one generation to the next and are also the first teachers of their offspring. As a result, most societal taboo begins with sexual taboo and primarily centers on fears of miscegenation, abandonment of culture, and degradation of the family unit. A woman's libido and reproduction must therefore be carefully controlled in order to maintain the integrity of the tribe or culture, defend the solidarity of their traditions, and pass this knowledge on to their children.

The underlying premise of this logic is the relationship between purity and pollution, the idea being that the woman is responsible for the maintenance of the established order through her actions, particularly those of a sexual nature. This type of thinking can be oppressive or uplifting, depending on one's philosophical orientation and social position within the tribe. Clearly, those who comply with the standards of the dominant culture can gain and maintain great status, while those who transgress the boundaries may find themselves outside of the protection of the system.

The radical element that Blavatsky entered into this dialogue is a concept of personal responsibility—shared equally by both genders—to contribute to and direct humankind's spiritual evolution. For the first time, women were empowered to participate and influence society for the greater good, regardless of their marital status and reproductive capabilities. Blavatsky reserved a special status for those without children, who are freed from domestic toil and therefore have the energy to devote themselves fully to the task of conscious evolution. This particular point is significant when one considers that the standard rhetoric of the time did much to disempower women outside of the typical family dynamic. Despite the racial constructions that proliferate her works, people were impressed by Blavatsky's charisma and accepted her attempts to offer an alternative construction of the world that appeared to not only resolve the conflicts between science and religion through the idea of rational magic, but also to unite men and women to work together to reinvigorate a disenchanted world.

Ironically, it appears that by including the prejudices of her time into her writing, Blavatsky was the first to successfully disseminate the progressive concept of sexual equality all over the world. Her theories of a universal esoteric truth at the heart of all religions of the world, rejection of the errors and crimes of the church as well as the perils of scientific materialism, and summons for humanity to utilize mystical and esoteric knowledge to participate in the conscious evolution of the soul, otherwise known as the Great Work, were abundantly appealing.

The gendered language and deterministic structure of Blavatsky's work capture the prevailing attitudes of her time, yet her radical concepts and alternative theology united the most progressive and ardent social reformers of the era. Feminism, vegetarianism, and labor reform are just a few of the political movements initiated by members of her Theosophical Society, many of whom went on to found esoteric orders of their own. As stated previously, not everyone was satisfied with the increasingly Eastern focus of Blavatsky's work, and many opted to construct separate occult societies with a distinctly Western orientation, mythology, and cultural context founded in Hermeticism.

Does utilizing a cultural construction of spirituality necessarily make one a racist? This valid question surfaces in discussions regarding race or cultural identity. Constructing cultural identity is not the equivalent of racism, although it often initially relies on a racial construction of self-identity. However, racism can easily become a byproduct of these philosophies, depending on the interpretation and subsequent actions of the audience. Much of Blavatsky's esoteric content is expressed in language that is racist by today's standards. While her work was not the cause of the endemic racism of the late 1800s, she certainly capitalized on it by giving it a spiritual framework.

A basic premise of Blavatsky's work is the pervasive mythology of the original, pure master race of the Atlanteans/Aryans amid a plethora of cursed sub-races. In this context, one's cultural consciousness is constantly vulnerable to pollution through interaction with less evolved beings. This became an undeniably popular theory of her time, as it justified and validated the eugenic aims of Western science, citing spiritual evolution as both the cause and concurrent answer to the problems of the day.

Due to the endemic influence of the Theosophical Society, many obscure as well as mainstream occult societies incorporated these beliefs into their own systems, filtering and tailoring them to express and validate their own convictions. Nazi occult theory is just one of many philosophies that was directly influenced by the racial constructions of spiritual evolution first popularized by Blavatsky's work, yet taken to extreme conclusions.

Does this connection invalidate the good deeds of the Theosophical Society and other organizations that were similarly inspired by her theories? Countless people were impressed by Blavatsky, and most were uninterested in a literal or violent interpretation of her philosophies. Many favored a figurative or allegorical interpretation of her more controversial topics and instead focused on the task of spiritual evolution through social and spiritual reform. Female enfranchisement and a revival of Christian esotericism are just a few of the movements also connected to these philosophies through the actions of women directly influenced by Blavatsky's work. Should these ideas be discarded because of their questionable theoretical origins? Of course not, but it is fruitful to analyze the source material to appreciate how it has been utilized to create harmony or destruction in the Modern Era, depending on its interpretation.

It is paramount to distinguish the difference between theory and practice. Although Blavatsky's words were later interpreted as theoretical justification for some dangerous and terrifying actions, her own personal actions prove that not only did she abhor violence, she greatly admired and advocated a kind of Mahayana Buddhism. She worked hard to improve conditions for those who were harmed by colonialism and create awareness about the resultant poverty in several countries, particularly India.

History is replete with examples of violent schisms and heresies that arise from different readings of the same religious texts, and the same words can inspire acts of great cruelty as well as kindness. Occult philosophy and esoteric discourse are not exempt from this trend, and it is important to acknowledge this fact. However, one of the advantages of esoteric discourse is that it is dynamic. Ideas that are clearly disadvantageous or dangerous can be abandoned, and what is useful may be retained and reinterpreted for positive results.

One concept that recurs frequently is that of two paths to spiritual enlightenment, the "open way" available to anyone and the path of renunciation for those who are childless through choice or circumstance. While both are viable options, Blavatsky (who was without children) postulated that renunciation was in some ways a deeper commitment, as freedom from domestic responsibilities allows for more energy to be turned to occult and religious study. Again, this concept of two paths serving to connect people with the Divine was appealing to women, especially for those not engaged in the traditional setup of marriage and family. Previously, there was no other socially acceptable option for women outside of marriage and motherhood, and unattached women were disenfranchised and regarded negatively.

The concept of renunciation afforded women the option of spiritual motherhood as a means of advancing the consciousness of her race or culture rather than its physical preservation. In her nonfiction, Dion Fortune adapts this idea of two paths toward spiritual enlightenment through her characterization of the hearthkeeper and that of the initiate. Bradley also describes a separate path for initiated priestesses as opposed to those with traditional families, though the term *renunciate* is reserved for her Darkover novels. Finally, Paxson makes a clear distinction between the traditional role of the priestess and that of the Lady of the Land, which is further explored in her solo work.

Blavatsky's construction of spiritual evolution and biological determinism influenced Fortune's works, who uses the concepts of "group soul" and "group mind" to offer an occult explanation of race and culture. Using a metaphor of a mountain, Fortune distinguishes the differences within the group soul as a series of crags upon the peak of humanity:

We further distinguish our own crag upon that peak from the crag of the negroes or the crag of the Chinese; and then come the finer distinctions that finally classify us into the Keltic, the Nordic, or the Latin sub-section, and we find ourselves definitely associated with others who have a certain temperamental and physical type in common. This is the biological foundation of our being, and we never get away from it.[95]

This description of the group soul is further defined as distinct from the concept of the group mind:

> The group soul is the raw material of mind-stuff out of which individual consciousness is differentiated by experience; the group mind is built out of the contributions of many individualized consciousnesses concentrating on the same ideas.[96]

If the group soul is the biological or genetic determinant of a unified people, the group mind is the culture or religion. If the group soul is the result of our nature, then the group mind is the result of our nurture. Fortune continues to postulate that it is this concept of the group mind which gives rise to occult secrecy, special costumes, and ritualistic practices:

> Anything which differentiates a number of individuals from the mass and sets them apart forms a group mind automatically. The more a group is segregated, the greater the difference between it and the rest of mankind, the stronger is the group mind thus engendered. Consider the group mind of the Jewish race, set apart by ritual, by manners, by temperament, and by persecution. There is nothing like persecution to give vitality to a group mind.

---

[95] Dion Fortune, *Society of the Inner Light Study Course No. I* (privately published, 1950), 72.
[96] Ibid., 76.

> Very truly is the blood of the martyrs the seed of the church, for it is the cement of the group mind.[97]

This importance of race to the cohesiveness of the group mind is prevalent throughout Fortune's works but also surfaces in the fictional works of Bradley and Paxson, with their emphasis on priestly castes and royal blood. Although the language has been updated and the word *culture* replaces the word *race* in the most recent books, the concept is the same. People become connected through custom, marriage, even hardship, and it is through this shared experience that cultures are created. They have babies together and become one race, or tribe.

There is nothing wrong with recognizing and celebrating solidarity with one's cultural identity. It is when these classifications become pejorative and are used to implement or justify social inequality that cultural theorizing becomes racism.

Sexual Dimorphism, Eugenics, and the Duty of the Priestess

The Law of Polarity, besides being understood as one of the theoretical bases for Western Esotericism, also has an application on the group model:

> The consciousness of a group is an entity of a negative or female type. It requires to be stimulated by a positive force before it can become creative. That which functions on a subtler plane is positive in relation to that which functions on a denser plane. Should a consciousness conceive the aims of a group on a higher plane than that on which the group conceives them, it becomes positive towards that group and thereby can fertilize it. When fertilization

---

97 Ibid., 78.

of a group occurs each of the individuals of that group becomes pregnant with a new life and brings creative work to birth upon the physical plane.[98]

This passage illustrates the fundamental reliance of Fortune's esoteric thought on the female/negative/below and male/positive/above distinctions, and it describes the role of the priestess as a fertilizing force on group consciousness. Without a grasp of this type of gendered construction, this passage (along with the bulk of the rest of her nonfiction work) becomes completely unintelligible.

It is similarly impossible to dismiss concepts of sexual dimorphism in the rest of the works reviewed in this study, as the subsequent authors embrace and promote this function of the priestess. Sex matters; the assignment of a body at birth links one into a complete hierarchal chain of being. In order for magic to work, there must be a fixed relationship or meaning for every sign in nature. The priestess, by virtue of her sex, has an obligation to accept her divine role as mother and therefore must be concerned with the evolution of her race/culture.

While Fortune's Moon Mistress is a spiritual mother concerned with the advancement of racial consciousness, Bradley's Witch Queen is a physical mother concerned with the preservation of the bloodline of the priestly caste. Paxson's Warrior Queen is also a mother, though she often chooses to promote the tribe or clan rather than solely the priestly caste, which often results in the assimilation of several cultures into a composite whole. A vital concern of early twentieth-century science, eugenic ideals

---

[98] Fortune, *The Cosmic Doctrine*, 161–162.

of building the "imperial race" were also of ultimate concern to concurrent esoteric discourse:

> In the argument that women's primary function was to be the mothers of a reinvigorated race, motherhood was redefined as a public and political function.[99]

The conservative Theosophical feminism of the "World Mother" movement of the late nineteenth and twentieth centuries accepted the sex-linked divisions of active/male/occultism and passive/female/mysticism popularized by the Liberal Catholic Church, proposing motherhood as the sacred duty of women that accomplishes both spiritual and material goals. This ideal is central to the works of Emily Lutyens, who proposes "woman's mission is to become the mother of future occultists—of those born without sin."[100]

Eugenics is the theory and practice of improving the genetic quality of humankind. This encompasses orchestrated breeding for desired traits, as well as population control through contraception and abortion. Women were at the forefront of this movement as well, as control over one's fertility is necessary for family planning and reducing overpopulation, which was a main concern of the time. Education was another concern, and many women appreciated the extra time to acquire degrees and pursue careers that a cessation in childbearing or even a child-free existence afforded them. Contraception is valued as a right of basic bodily integrity that is up to the individual to eschew or implement as she sees fit. Many women felt that this freedom to choose

---

99   Dixon, 214.
100 Ibid., 212.

when to access their own fertility was the very thing that would afford cultural and spiritual evolution, as there would be no more unwanted children in the world, or at least less of them. Women could then turn their attention to better nurturing their present children or abstaining from motherhood altogether if they so desired.

However, another goal of eugenics is to suppress the fertility of so-called undesirable populations. There are many notable studies pertaining to the forced sterilization and administration of contraceptives to indigenous populations, the poor, the disabled, and the incarcerated in massive experiments, oftentimes without informed consent. Eugenics advocates the encouragement of desirable traits through perfectly controlled fertility, but also the eradication of unwanted traits through prescriptive sterility. This controversial topic continues to surface in contemporary culture and is also a recurring theme in esoteric fiction.

While Fortune overtly disassociates her characters Earth Mother and Moon Mistress from eugenic connotations by presenting them as childless, the subtext of her work does imply that a rigorous selective breeding program was enacted in Atlantis to fix and preserve the psychic gifts of the ruling priestly class. Bradley's Witch Queen is both the product and promoter of eugenics, as the sacred bloodline of Avalon must be preserved at all costs. (Outside of the Avalon series, eugenics is also a prime concern of the inhabitants of Darkover in order to preserve their psychic abilities.) Paxson's Warrior Queen is also concerned with maintaining the bloodline of her tribe, but the combination of different races/ cultures is often presented as having positive results and is shown to unlock and strengthen latent magical ability in the offspring.

Although the intermingling of the people is often accompanied by war and strife, the gist of Paxson's work is that the combination of the various tribes is inevitable and ultimately serves the gods. However, unplanned pregnancy is often presented as a disaster, and abortion is a valid alternative to bearing an unwanted child.

Sacrifice and the Sword

All of the authors analyzed in this study retain the destructive power associated with the Salome image in their conceptions of priestess and Goddess. Fortune's Moon Mistress is a reincarnated Atlantean adept who formerly specialized in human sacrifices. Bradley's Witch Queen swiftly executes those she perceives as threats or traitors to the Goddess tradition.[101] Paxson's Warrior Queen uses both magic and weapons to defend herself and her tribe. This image of the priestess as warrior is not discordant with the theme of the priestess as mother, as all three authors ascribe dominion over life and death to the Goddess. The priestess as warrior is the aggressive defender of the spiritual and physical well-being of her race/culture; similarly, the Warrior/Dark Mother aspect of the Goddess is a dynamic, brutal force that is aroused when the sacred harmony is disturbed.

She is the woman with the sword, priestess and warrior. Man's severed head is offered as a symbol of the initiatory death that leads to the gnosis and wisdom that accompanies an acceptance of and surrender to the divine feminine. The image can also imply the physical and spiritual death reserved for those who refuse to

---

101 Bradley, MA 673: Morgaine calls on the Dark Mother to kill a political threat; MA 763: Morgaine sends Nimue to seduce Kevin and bring him back to Avalon for execution.

acknowledge her power and mistreat her human counterparts. The sword is the physical representation of this power. Bradley's interpretation of this concept is Excalibur, the sacred sword of Avalon, which is granted to Arthur as a pledge of his fealty to the Goddess religion.[102] Conflict arises when Arthur swears a Christian oath on the sword, and Morgaine demands that he render it back to Avalon.[103] The phallic sword, symbol of Arthur's kingship and power, is his only so long as he honors the divine feminine; when he begins to endorse patriarchal Christianity to the people, the priestess seeks to reclaim it in the name of the Goddess.[104]

Paxson presents the sword as a physical symbol of sovereignty granted only through the grace of the Goddess, but she adds a twist to the concept of the sacrificial king by allowing the queen to take the king's place if he is unable to fulfill his oath to die for the land. Each of her stories used for this analysis features some kind of example of a character, male or female, sacrificing themselves for a perceived wrong. In *Ancestors of Avalon*, Deoris elects to stay behind on the sinking island to atone for her part in the destruction of Atlantis.[105] In *Ravens of Avalon*, Boudica is sacrificed to atone for her part in the Celtic defeat and to fulfill her oath.[106] Finally, in *Sword of Avalon*, Velentos characterizes his death as a necessary sacrifice to clean the taint of the traitor's touch from the sacred blade Excalibur.[107]

---

102 MA 203.
103 MA 717.
104 MA 732–747.
105 AA 52.
106 RA 389.
107 SA 407.

The priestess in twentieth-century fiction is a revolutionary figure. She heralds a new direction in Western esoteric thought because she presents an alternative construction of woman as both worldly and divine. Yet she is never completely free of patriarchal associations and bias because she is a product of them. All of the authors reviewed in this study employ the language and characterization of feminine evil in their presentation of the priestess. However, although the priestess is dependent on these constructions for her initial existence, her catalytic nature contains the potential to transcend them.

Feminine Evil in the Works of Dion Fortune

Although Fortune's fictional works are most memorable for their emphasis on the divine and redemptive powers of the feminine, she acknowledges the commonly held perceptions of feminized evil of her time and confirms their place in the modern context. However, Fortune's conception of feminine evil, instead of being characterized by the traditional motifs of angel/demon and spinster/whore, is represented almost exclusively throughout her novels as the sisters, mothers, and wives of the male protagonists.

This theme is apparent in the opening scenes of *The Goat Foot God*, as Hugh Patson's late wife, Frida, is personified as treacherous and gold-digging, having had an illicit affair for years with his cousin.[108] His mother and sister are continually depicted as greedy, ganging up against him in order to secure his inheritance for their own interests, going so far as to enlist the family doctor in a scheme to get him certified.[109] This motif is echoed in

---

108 GFG 40.
109 Ibid., 194.

Sea Priestess, where the villains are Wilfred Maxwell's mother and sister, who successfully prevent him from selling the family business and home through badgering and whining, and are assisted by a fortuitous asthma attack on his part. Wilfred's sister, Ethel, is depicted as a vicious shrew who repeatedly nags her brother throughout the text and eventually slanders his reputation, as well as that of Molly Coke, his bride-to-be.[110] The last example of feminine evil in Fortune's fiction is personified by the character of Eva, Rupert Malcolm's wife in *Moon Magic*. Introduced as an invalid from the unsuccessful birth of their child, she shuns her husband's presence and all physical contact with him. After her death, toward the end of the story, it is revealed that she faked the whole illness as an excuse to live apart from him, so as not to be bothered with conjugal obligations.[111]

Fortune inverts the standard narrative of model womanhood of her time. She depicts socially acceptable roles of womanhood, such as mother/sister/wife and women's groups such as the Girl's Friendly, in a way that contradicts their positive associations and instead presents them as sources of the worst kinds of repression. Her spectrum of feminine evil encompasses promiscuity, deceit, greed, jealousy, slander, and frigidity—all traits that serve to emasculate the male protagonists of her novels. The worst wounds inflicted upon the male psyche are typically associated with sexual dysfunction and often stem from being denied sexual or emotional intimacy. An unhappy marriage is seen as the source of most of these societal ills; although she endorses marriage as

---

110   SP 2–3, 198–199.

111   MM 203.

the only legitimate setup between men and women toward the end of *The Goat Foot God*[112], the end of *Moon Magic* concludes with an entirely different proposition offered by le Fay that belies this earlier stance:

> I can give your manhood fulfillment—more than you can possibly dream or believe, even though you cannot possess me. I'd like to show you what a woman can be to a man. You deserve it. You've been starved so long…that is how it is with us who are initiates. It is different with us from what it is with the once-born, for we belong in Another Place…You have got to live in this world, and I have got to live in two worlds, and this is the best I can offer you—I will mate with you after another manner—coming and going in my own way…I will make you happy but you mustn't try to possess me.

To which Malcolm replies, "Possession is a strong instinct with some men. It's their notion of love." Lilith asserts:

> It's a false notion. No one can possess another without destroying them. That is why marriages are such makeshifts. The one is only partly satisfied, the other is half destroyed. The far-voyaging soul must be free, coming and going in its own sphere. Let us learn to love as those love who are free from the Wheel of Birth and Death.[113]

This love that the priestess is proposing is, in a sense, free love, unrestricted by societal taboo or obligation. It is offered as a corrective to the stunting, smothering types of love displayed by her myriad female foils. Even though the sublimation of sexual forces in acts of magic is one of the main characteristics of Fortune's

---

112   GFG 311.
113   MM 233–234.

works, careful reading of the last few pages of *Moon Magic* seems to indicate the novel's culmination is a ritualistic sexual consummation between the two protagonists.[114] This reversal of her earlier stance, although veiled in mysterious terminology and innuendo, completes Fortune's ideal of the priestess and her conception of modern womanhood. This is a woman who is sexually empowered, with the power to love or hold herself apart as she sees fit, who lives by her own moral code but does not infringe or impose on that of another. She is a woman whose power is dependent on her own merit and the knowledgeable cooperation of her male counterparts; this power is not acquired through the emasculation or promiscuous sexual manipulation of the men in her life.

Feminine Evil in the Works of Marion Zimmer Bradley

The priestess's sexual freedom is countermanded by a convoluted set of sexual laws and taboo in Bradley's works. Ironically, Fortune reserves the type of sexual freedom to love as one wills for the initiated few, while in Bradley's text this right is most easily invoked by those with no caste ties to the priestesshood. This convention is illustrated in the seemingly contradictory customs of the priestly caste in *The Fall of Atlantis*:

> A woman had this right, under the Law, and indeed in the old days it had been rare for a woman to marry before she had proven her womanhood by bearing a child to the man of her choice.

---

114   MM 236–241.

Contrasted with the statement on the next page:

> A woman might choose a lover, but if she and her affianced husband possessed one another before marriage, it was considered a terrible disgrace; such haste and precipitancy would be cause enough for dismissing both from the Acolytes.[115]

While choice of sexual partner is considered a fundamental freedom, nonreproductive sex and promiscuous behavior are not endorsed by the religion of the Witch Queen. Hildebrand notes that in *Mists of Avalon* "Bradley links evil with female sexuality"[116] and asserts that the characters of Morgause and Gwenhwyfar represent the traditional patriarchal associations of open sexuality and the evil woman, and that their sexuality is emphasized more than other female characters.[117] Fortune's evil connotations of the faithless wife are reproduced in Bradley's works; however, Bradley extends these negative connotations to include nonreproductive heterosexual magic.

While the priestess is presented as the epitome of sacred sexuality and fertility magic, the image of the sorceress, who uses sex for occult purposes and avoids pregnancy, is presented as unnatural and perverse and epitomizes sexual evil. Morguase is the sorceress in *Mists of Avalon*; promiscuous and cunning, her political scheming culminates in a human sacrifice that grants her magical power.[118] However, homosexuality is not negatively portrayed in Bradley's texts; even though it is a form of nonreproductive sex, it is instead characterized as a healing and sacramental act.[119]

---

115 FA 171–172.
116 Hildebrand, 121.
117 Ibid., 121–122.
118 MA 817.
119 Raven romantically welcomes Morgaine back to Avalon, MA 640; Arthur, Lancelot, and Gwenhwyfar share a bed at Beltane, MA 448.

This division between priestess and sorceress is most evident in Bradley's *Fall of Atlantis*. Sisters Domaris and Deoris represent these two polarities of the female experience in Bradley's works. Born to the highest priestly caste of Atlantis, the sisters are reared in the Temple of Light. Domaris becomes an initiated Priestess of the Light, but Deoris breaks caste law and instead chooses the Gray Temple and the Magician's path, and learns techniques of sexual magic forbidden to those of the priestly caste.[120] Except for Deoris, who is the pupil and lover of the head magician, Riveda, and Maleina, the only fully trained female magician, all of the women associated with the Gray Temple represent Bradley's assessment of the ultimate degradation of the feminine and sexual evil. The *saji* are outcast women who undergo a dangerous and intensely sexual training that results in advanced psychic development. The process does not always yield results, but even if successful the *saji* are still considered nonhuman, sexual accessories to be used by the magicians in occult rituals.[121] The sadomasochistic characterization of the relationship between Deoris and Riveda, and those of the male and female members of the Gray Temple, illustrates Bradley's opinion of the gender dynamics of mid-twentieth century occultism and represents nonreproductive sexuality as blasphemous and life-negating. The unsanctioned sexual and magical experimentation of Deoris and Riveda culminates in a sacrilegious rite that is ultimately responsible for the destruction of the continent,[122] while the actions taken by Domaris to reconsecrate both sisters to the Mother Goddess

---

120 Bradley, FA 264.
121 "One girl in four, when she reached puberty, went into raving madness and died of convulsive nerve spasms." FA 300.
122 FA 338.

are credited with preserving the remnants of the Atlantean race and culture.[123] In essence, female sexuality that is sublimated for occult effect destroys Atlantis, while motherhood saves it.

As motherhood is central to Bradley's characterization of the divine feminine, abortion is negatively portrayed and often not an option for the priestess. Fortune condemns abortion in her fictional works and, for the most part, Bradley agrees with this sentiment, although with some qualifiers. Abortion is illegal in Atlantean society; even though the child Deoris is carrying was conceived in a blasphemous rite and is possibly the incarnation of a demonic god, she is not granted the option of terminating the pregnancy, even if it is an abomination.[124] In *The Firebrand*, Kassandra is brutally raped during the sack of Troy and then kidnapped, to be treated in the same rough manner almost to the point of death. Kassandra ceases to be abused when it is discovered that she is pregnant. Although she intends to acquire the necessary herbs to induce miscarriage, her captivity prevents this, and she is forced to carry the child to term.[125]

Morgaine in *Mists of Avalon* is similarly forbidden to abort her child once she discovers it is the product of incest. Conceived in the Great Marriage, the child is considered holy and is the realization of the eugenic breeding program of the head priestess, Viviane, to produce a sacred king for Avalon.[126] Morgaine concedes and carries the pregnancy to term, but she later aborts an unwanted child when she believes herself too old to bear it safe-

---

123 FA 267, 441–444.
124 FA 417–418.
125 FB 578.
126 MA 228.

ly.[127] This action is linked in the text with the death of her lover, Accolon, and the wreck of her political plans. Bradley implies that while woman has the power of life and death, the priestess, as a representative of the Goddess, must choose life or suffer karmic consequences.

This priestess/sorceress polarity parallels the dichotomy of Bradley's Mother Goddess in her light and dark aspects. Feminine evil is sacralized in Bradley's texts and grafted into the persona of the Goddess, who is often blamed for the priestesses' most ruthless actions and decisions: "It was not I that was cruel, but the Goddess."[128] This is a theoretical shift from Fortune's Black/White Isis, who is presented as the divine opposite of Fortune's characterization of feminine evil. Unlike her predecessors, Earth Mother and Moon Mistress, Witch Queen's power is completely dependent upon her sexuality. As a priestess and warrior, sex is both her sacred duty and weapon of choice.

Feminine Evil in the Works of Diana L. Paxson

Paxson's approach to characterizing female identity is different than that of her predecessors in several ways. First, she attempts to be inclusive of all women. Typically there is not a clearly defined evil woman in the text. While there is strife and personality conflicts between characters, there is always an accompanying explanation that describes each character's point of view. Even villains, such as Galid in *Sword of Avalon*, are not simply characterized as "bad guys." There is a pathology behind his crimes

---

127   MA 737.
128   MA 140.

that stems from loneliness and despair. This device is also applied to unsavory females in the texts, so even incoherently malicious actions tend to be mitigated by circumstance. While this approach does not exonerate the characters, it does lead the reader to consider that each character has complex reasons that contribute to their choices.

This tendency to avoid absolutism is one of the definitive departures of Paxson's work from the other authors reviewed here. The priestess's core values and absolute ethics are often challenged in the texts and may be mitigated or even abandoned if they become obsolete. This can be due to external factors, such as war and migration, or internal factors, such as political strife and personal choice. The result is that the priestess is presented as making decisions in a world devoid of absolute values, often without a clear distinction between right and wrong, in the midst of chaotic change. Practicality often wins out over tradition. Consequently, Paxson presents scenarios and outcomes that are widely divergent from those of previous authors.

One example of the theme of inclusiveness is the reintroduction of the *saji*—women sworn to serve the Gray Temple and the magicians of Atlantis—in *Ancestors of Avalon*. Despite Bradley's extensive negative portrayal of these women in *Fall of Atlantis*, in Paxson's story they are granted a new image and status working alongside the other Atlantean survivors. When acolytes of the Temple of Light express aversion of having to work with the women, they are chided for believing the *saji* are "mindless Temple whores."[129] While their proficiency in sex magic is noted as a valid path to enlightenment, it is their skill in herbal lore that

---

129   AA 134.

is prized in the new land. There is no further reference to the *saji* or their former role in Atlantean society in the text; they are presented simply as industrious women working alongside the other survivors. One may infer that this brief cameo is a deliberate attempt to neutralize Bradley's earlier negative characterization of the *saji* and, by extension, classical sex magic. However, the subject of sex magic is abandoned entirely, and the ecstatic techniques of the *saji* are not speculated upon or incorporated into the new worship. This silence shows that there is a distinction between Atlantean sex magic and the sacred rites of Avalon, although this is not explicitly stated in the text.

Another example of this trend is the character of Cartimandua in *Ravens of Avalon*. Ruling queen of the tribes of Brigantes, she is Lhiannon's contemporary and was her fellow student in the House of Maidens. She is presented as frank, ambitious, and lusty from an early age, as Lhiannon remembers her taking many lovers before she was officially allowed to participate in the Beltane rites.[130] Each time that Cartimandua is introduced in the text, there is some mention of her promiscuity. This is accompanied with a reference to the Brigantes having "different ways," with their women exercising a political power and sexual freedom that is unknown to the other clans.

Cartimandua is a minor character in the story, yet she is responsible for two major developments in the plot. First, she inspires the inebriated Boudica to flee her wedding feast after relaying her own tribal customs of having the groom prove his virility by catching his bride-to-be.[131] While this action does not

---

130   RA 102.
131   RA 120.

inspire outright hostility between the pair, it does damage her husband's reputation when he is unable to accomplish this task, and the marriage begins with uncertainty.

The second action that affects the story is that Cartimandua turns in the leader of the rebel forces, Caratac, to the Romans.[132] As he is also the sworn defender of the Britannia, this action is considered a betrayal, although it does, in fact, spare his life. Catarac becomes a hostage and joins his family to live in Rome, and becomes neutralized as a threat to Roman rule. This event sets the stage for Boudica to later be named Lady of the Land and to take his place as the sacrifice when she is unable to succeed as defender.

Cartinmadua's influence is present in both of these pivotal events. Again, Paxson does not overtly present Cartimandua as an evil woman, but the little information that is revealed about this character is that she is ambitious, promiscuous, and often wields a negative influence on the events and people around her. The reader is left to draw their own conclusions.

Fidelity is a core concept in Paxson's construction of the priestess, despite the sexual freedom that is supposedly available to her. Temptation may occur, but she typically resists. The women who invoke sexual freedom are often unmarried or not yet pledged to serve the Goddess. Another recurring theme is that of a priestess so focused on her work that she has little time or desire to seek out sex or companionship. Years may pass, the spouse or male counterpart may be absent or prove unfaithful or even die, and yet the priestess often remains faithful and unpartnered for the rest of her life. While it is clear that promiscuity is not encour-

---

132   RA 230.

aged by the standards of Avalon, celibacy and extended virginity are similarly discouraged unless there is some spiritual or magical purpose to achieve. Abstinence is discussed from a new perspective in Paxson's work, and several of her priestesses refrain from sexual contact altogether. Again, the emphasis is on personal choice, and the priestess remains the ultimate authority of her bodily integrity.

Sexual freedom and orientation is presented as the sole decision of the priestess, which trumps tradition in almost every scenario. This is most evident in the choices of Tirilan in *Sword of Avalon*, particularly the scenes wherein she offers her body to tame the fury of her captor, Galid. She ransoms herself for the safety of her people, saying "If I will love you, freely and without force, will you let Azan go?"[133] Despite her circumstances, this is not presented as a desperate act but instead is described as an offer of healing and redemption. Tirilan's love is her greatest asset, and instead of offering aggression she seeks to mitigate the war by offering herself in surrender. This logic exemplifies the importance of personal perspective to the dialogue and displays that the actions of the Warrior Queen are always dependent on her circumstances rather than absolute values.

Rather than presenting evil characters, Paxson defines evil through actions or poor choices that result from various character flaws, such as pride, anger, and jealousy. Even the rage of the Morrigan is characterized as a reflection of the limitations of the priestesses that invoke her. The emphasis is always on personal choice, and the results are subject to interpretation.

---

133   SA 349, 357.

The final aspect of Warrior Queen's philosophy that is most divergent from her predecessors is her stance on abortion. Unlike Fortune and Bradley, Paxson does not present this act as inherently evil or as a sin against the Goddess. In fact, the priestesses in her works are often presented as possessing the sacred knowledge of the herbs and techniques that will terminate undesirable pregnancy. This is considered a natural and necessary function of the midwife's role, as the Goddess has dominion over life and death, and is included in the priestess training.

Fortune does not delve too far into this topic in her fiction, instead advocating contraception as an ethical means to avoid pregnancy, but she is opposed to abortion in her occult nonfiction. While there is little occult nonfiction available from Bradley, her stance on this issue is clearly against both contraception and abortion. Paxson takes the opposite view and is an adamant supporter of family planning and abortion, but this is not surprising given the importance of choice to her concept of priestess and Goddess.

As Paxson's characters are often reigning queens and preservation of the tribal blood is paramount, abortion would be seem to be counterproductive to this goal. However, abortion is posited as a sacred right available to every female as an extension of the Goddess. This conflict of interest is resolved as the protagonist never seems to take advantage of this option herself but endorses it as a viable course of action for others. Abortion is presented as a regrettable event that is sometimes necessary to prevent future suffering. This concept is most clearly defined in *Ravens of Avalon*, where Lhiannon offers to help fellow priestess Coventa abort a child conceived by rape. Coventa refuses, and Lhiannon is shocked, thinking:

I would tear out my womb rather than bear a Roman's child! Coventa will not be the only one burdened this way...Perhaps the other women will be more sensible, and if they cannot kill the babies before they are born, they will destroy them after.[134]

Coventa later dies giving birth to the child. Lhiannon's prediction becomes a reality as the other priestesses raped in the attack drown the resultant female children and raise the sons to become rebels against Rome.[135] This proposal of abortion as an alternative to infanticide exemplifies the stark pragmatism that dictates the philosophy of Paxson's priestess and the complexity of her image of the Goddess.

The priestess in esoteric fiction is both a political and religious ideal. She presents the image of a sanctified woman who is a servant of the Goddess. She uses her personal and sexual power to promote the aims of her tribe and tradition. The sorceress is the foil of the priestess. She often works outside of the established paradigm and utilizes her sexuality in a way that is unsanctioned by the ethics of the priestess and tribe. However, the morality of the priestess is fluid, dependent upon the time in which she is created, not necessarily the time in which her story is set. Sometimes the priestess utilizes the methods of the sorceress and can even be the same character, depending on the situation. The Goddess is similarly depicted as both kind and cruel, personal and remote, implacable and persuasive all at once. This paradox is the core of the catalytic nature of this concept of woman as both priestess and Goddess.

---

134   RA 339–340.
135   RA 390.

It is the priestess's flawed nature that makes her such an accessible character. Fortune's character smokes, drives too fast, reveals information when and if it suits her purpose, and is not above faking her own death to avoid uncomfortable interpersonal explanations of her actions. Bradley's characters are often judgmental, absolutely convinced of their own righteousness, and display a stunning lack of foresight when it comes to family relationships. Paxson's characters are similarly arrogant, jealous, overworked to the point of exhaustion, and make poor decisions when inebriated. All of the characters proclaim themselves to be sexually liberated, but none approve of women taking multiple lovers or exercising sexual freedoms foreign to the customs of the priestess. Each character is capable of great cruelty in the pursuit of her goals and then finds some kind of reason, no matter how tenuous, to excuse her actions.

Yet these traits are exactly why the character of the priestess is so compelling. She is human. She makes mistakes. She falls in love at the wrong time and sometimes makes poor choices. She is judgmental. Her perseverance in the face of adversity and ability to transcend her own failings is why this motif has endured for so long in esoteric fiction. The depiction of the Goddess in these texts as both light and dark, salvific and terrifying at the same time is one that is intensely mysterious and continues to fascinate. The priestess—and, by extension, the Goddess—is dynamic because she harnesses power that is both sacred and profane to challenge her own limitations and transmute them into strength.

Chapter 9

NEW FRONTIERS

THIS CHAPTER CONTAINS my personal thoughts on the related images of the priestess and Goddess. Although personal experience is a key component to authenticity, it is difficult to take that first step and discuss one's private perspective in a public forum; however, this is a necessary step in starting any dialogue. This chapter is provided to give some context to several topics discussed in this book, as well as my recommendations on new directions for future research. Its intent is to encourage introspection and facilitate the art of sharing one's experience with others.

On Ordeals

Any author will identify with the idea that writing a book is an ordeal. Some endeavors are so consuming that they have almost a corrosive effect on their creators—old ideas and attitudes dissolve in order for something new to materialize. This is not a comfortable process, but it is educational. These lessons are in many ways the most valuable. The knowledge they impart is extremely precious, as it is not easily won. *The Priestess and the Pen* has been this kind of book. Much of the research began very long ago and has been compounded with time. It has been concluded in the midst of raising toddlers and the regular chaos of family life. There are passages that have flowed as smooth as honey and others that have been agony to produce. At times the content has been both fascinating and repellent to me. This has not been an easy book to create, but the experience has been incredible. I have been extremely fortunate to have met and worked with some fantastic people to bring this project to life, and I feel blessed to be able to share it.

However, this experience has forced me to scrutinize many aspects of my own faith and philosophy, which is not a pleasant task. Plus, researching the historical origins of anything one really cares about will definitely result in uncovering some uncomfortable truths as preconceived notions are proven false. For myself, discovering that many of the ideas I have embraced and found some truth in have been similarly used by others to endorse personal actions and policies that I find repugnant was a difficult revelation. I wondered if the well itself was poisoned, for if others could attempt to justify their actions with these theories, where would these thoughts lead me?

It is difficult to let go of the concept of the incorruptible hero, or a perfect ideal that cannot be misused, even when confronted with historical facts that prove otherwise. Yet in order to preserve these concepts and history for posterity, one has to embrace both the bitter and the sweet and accept that no one owns an idea. The power of an idea is proven by its ability to shape history through its various interpretations, both positive and negative, as well as its endurance. In order for us to claim the lessons of history, we must be willing to accept these facts and admit that philosophies and religion can be used by anyone to justify their own desires. It is up to the individual to reflect their version of the ideal and remember that one's actions are a distinct, personal choice.

Dig deep enough into the origins of most esoteric groups and philosophies, and you will find that there is always some murky beginning that involves good people working alongside unsavory personalities, founded on revelations of questionable authenticity. Does this mean that the work and theories they espouse are meaningless? Absolutely not. The important point is the effect that these symbols have on the audience and the subsequent actions that person takes. Is the concept rejected or is it entertained, even accepted? How these ideals are realized, whether they are used to promote positive actions or espouse junk philosophy, is determined by the individual.

Ultimately we are the ones who bring meaning to our lives through the use of the imagination. In my opinion, it comes down to a personal choice between indifference or empowerment. Are we victims of circumstance—random specks floating in a meaningless void—or do we assign some sort of lesson to the events of our lives and salvage something from each episode? I choose the latter and am responsible for translating the raw experience of my life into something more. I am the author of my own experience. I can use whatever language and methods that best accomplish this goal.

This realization has both positive and negative aspects. While it is empowering to live a life that is self-directed, it is daunting to fly without a net. To know thyself, it is imperative to develop the skill of becoming a critical thinker without losing a sense of wonder. The imagination is the greatest gift that humans share; it is the key to our salvation or damnation. While the ability to suspend disbelief is sometimes necessary in order to achieve empowerment, the task of knowing oneself is not always a positive endeavor. It should not be easy; in fact, if it is an honest effort, it is an ordeal.

Negative feelings and uncomfortable realizations are part of the process. It is important to recognize one's limitations as well as one's strengths in order to translate experience into something new. Remember that there is a difference between honesty and self-abuse, and it is easy to get depressed or stuck in a negative loop. Education begins with self-analysis, but it does not end there. Learn as much as possible, and constantly provide the mind with fresh material in order to keep it resilient enough to handle the grueling task of introspection. Without exposing the mind to new information, how can you gauge whether you have reached an epiphany or a dead end? It is so easy to get lazy, and mental complacency is the thief of all motivation.

This is why it is so important to preserve and maintain interest in the study of the humanities. Despite current propaganda that declares subjects such as liberal arts, philosophy, and religious studies are useless to pursue, in fact, the exact opposite is true. Humanities and related subjects give us perspective on the history of ideas. They teach us that different philosophies are connected and how this affects the cultures and politics of the world we live in. Understanding how human imagination has changed the world is always useful. It invigorates the mind, refreshes the soul, and stimulates the senses.

Abandonment of these concepts is nonproductive, causing despondency and cultural stagnation. Unfortunately, as education is progressively consumer driven and tailored for success in the corporate world, more people are getting swindled into thinking that avoiding or discarding these subjects entirely will somehow be advantageous in the long run, as if the mind is some finite library with limited shelf space available for new information. Arts and humanities classes are routinely cut or eliminated in public education in order to promote some sort of new methodology or other experimental approach.

Yet it appears as if the human mind actually thrives when stimulated and can accommodate vast amounts of knowledge and experience while still maintaining the ability to master new technologies. As always, it is up to the individual to direct the course of one's education. Stale thoughts will breed boring minds. Keep yours fresh, and mix it up with subjects that you would not typically pursue. Without the benefit of outside information, much of the knowledge gleaned from introspection is impossible to sort out in a constructive way. The nature of experience is that it is emotionally charged, and exposure to the stories and philosophies of others grants a perspective that is highly useful. This in turn provides a better understanding of the self in comparison with others who have struggled with the same questions throughout history.

Beyond the Triple Goddess

Another disconcerting byproduct of analyzing the origin of the priestess in the modern era is the realization that the concept of the Triple Goddess can become extremely limiting when it becomes dogma. This is not an easy thing to state, as this image has been venerated by many, including myself. Although my first introduction to the Triple Goddess was through fiction, there were several other authors who proposed alternative constructions that held equal appeal. One notable fourfold representation of the Goddess can be found in the works of Mercedes Lackey. Many others depicted various goddesses in their stories, which changed with the region or location of the tale. I accepted early on that different people relate to her in different ways, so it seemed natural to work with whatever form felt right to me.

When I began actively exploring Paganism and Wicca in my twenties, I was reintroduced to the concept of the Triple Goddess through the nomenclature of other like-minded folks. People were happy to share their thoughts and experiences of the Triple Goddess, and there were many long conversations concerning her nature. While many people embraced this concept, there were few who could claim that their own lives conformed to this pattern. For some this is not a problem; but for others, particularly women, this disconnect may create a feeling of internal dissonance when their lives do not mirror the ideal. It has become apparent to me that any religious ideal, even alternative ones, can be internalized in unwholesome ways. When the interpretation becomes literal, adherence to the form precludes evolution of the concept.

Just as there is a difference between theory and practice, there is a gap between the icon of the Triple Goddess and its application to the stages of a woman's life. While the attempt to honor different aspects of the aging process is commendable, the icon is somewhat disconnected from many folks's actual experience.

Many women do not have children, by choice or otherwise, and therefore face the challenge of attempting to incorporate an ideal that does not reflect their physical reality. The result is an abstract image of the Divine that is not immediately accessible to many of her followers on a personal level. How does the woman without children fit in with the depiction of the Triple Goddess? She can worship but never replicate the divine pattern. Her actual life experience finds no counterpart in the image held up as divine.

The main problem with the concept is that it begins by glorifying the biological functions of reproduction and aging as the key determinants that provide meaning in a woman's life, namely youth, fecundity, and sterility. This idea is translated as the Maiden, Mother, and Crone, and it is used to describe the Goddess as well as her human counterparts. (Though utilizing the term *wisewoman* or *sage* is often a polite alternative to the word *crone* when referring to a priestess.) While other esoteric traits are attributed to each of the three faces, the main idea starts from an assumption of sexual dimorphism that is ageist, as there are cultural expectations of a woman's actions assigned to each of the three states. Unsurprisingly, these ideas of acceptable behavior include stereotypes of sexual behavior and taboo that echo assumptions of the dominant narrative. This is fine if one's experience corresponds with the pattern, but it becomes problematical when it does not. The labels no longer apply and can be misleading.

My first experience of this began when I was a young woman. Other Pagans would often comment that my "Maiden energy" was strong. When I asked them to describe what they meant, often this was explained as a compliment to my enthusiasm and physical appearance. I emanated Maiden energy simply because of my age and the reaction that I inspired in others. My personal experience was not factored into these pronouncements. If I disclosed the fact that I instead felt a stronger internal resonance with Crone energy, the standard response was often surprise and disbelief. Usually I would receive some kind of qualification: my feelings were "some other facet of the Maiden" or outright denial. It was of no consequence that this was not the way I chose to identify myself. Although I was busy forming study groups and embarking on a path of formal spiritual discipline, I was simply too young to be viewed as anything but a maiden. No longer an individual but instead a symbol. I had a role to play: it was assigned to me by virtue of my age and gender, and others would view my actions through this lens.

Throughout my twenties this idea was strengthened through several unpleasant interactions with strangers who did not know me personally but had seen me at a festival or participating in some other public event and felt the need to approach me with their unsolicited opinions and advice. It seemed as if folks had formed such a strong attachment to the image they had created for the "Maiden" that they held no reservations whatsoever of informing me of their expectations or disappointment with my behavior as a representative of the Goddess. These interactions left me feeling objectified and disheartened.

These people were not interested in knowing me—they were merely imparting whatever comment they wished to share. The message typically described how I was either affirming or denying their conviction of what Maiden energy represented to them. Most of them did not even know my name. The repetitive nature of these episodes taught me a corollary lesson: that people see what they have been conditioned to accept. Regardless of my personal feelings on the matter, the community would deal with me in a manner that reinforced their own perceptions.

I have found that this dissonance continues into my thirties, otherwise known as my Mother stage. When I was pregnant with my first child, I attended a workshop in which we were supposed to do a brainstorming exercise of concepts associated with the Triple Goddess. My group was assigned the Mother, and we began tossing ideas around. One of the thoughts I shared was my new perspective on pregnancy and sexual awareness. Although the Maiden is usually billed as the sexy one of the three facets of the Goddess and held up as a symbol of sexual liberation, my personal experience was quite different. As a result of pregnancy, my hormones had shifted in such a way that my libido had markedly increased. I was now connected to my body and its responses in such a way that sex took on a new depth and greater intensity than ever before. I proposed that "sexy" be added to our list of Mother attributes.

When it was time to share our comments, a respected elder in the Pagan community who was leading the workshop informed me that "sexy" is not associated with the Mother but is instead a quality of the Maiden. The Mother, it seems, is no longer interested in starting new life but instead focuses her energies on nurturing and sustaining her tribe. It was also announced that the Crone has moved beyond these concerns of the flesh as well, unless she is emoting Maiden energy. I found this explanation extremely amusing and completely disconnected from reality. I have known grandmothers who are outrageous flirts and proud of it, happily past the green modesty of youth. Divorcing sexual desire from the idea of fecundity (or wisdom) is just bizarre. If sex is natural and healthy, then it stands to reason that it should be considered a nurturing and healing force, even for a mature individual.

The problem begins by assigning sexual attractiveness as one of the main characteristics of the Maiden. This line of thinking only reinforces the dominant narrative's equation of youth with beauty and serves to objectify our daughters with confusing rhetoric. Likewise, the other two facets seemed stripped of their own share of the beauty and power of sex, which is reminiscent of the limitations of the dominant narrative.

It seemed apparent to me that the conventional image of the Triple Goddess did not fit in with my experience and needed enhancement. Rather than trying to tack on an explanation of sexuality in relation to the other three faces, I felt that a woman's sexual identity and passion necessitate a separate aspect. I noticed that others were already doing this in some form, by either adopting a personal deity to worship or supplementing their concept of the Triple Goddess with separate aspects of different goddesses. There is a precedent of experimentation with this topic in esoteric fiction, as the image of the Goddess in the West has never been static and has evolved over time. She is revolutionary, the initiator of female political power in the modern era, and therefore correlates on some level with the actual experience of her followers. The key component is the Priestess, who is the activating principle and the fourth face of the Goddess.

To me, the idea of a fourfold Divine makes much more sense. There are four seasons, four elements, four cardinal directions, and four phases of the moon. The addition of another facet to the

Triple Goddess serves to validate and personalize an otherwise abstract ideal. The number three is transcendental, but the number four symbolizes manifestation. While the Maiden, Mother, and Crone are basic descriptions of the biological potential of most women, the fourth face is her key to personal power and self-identity. This is the facet that incorporates her actual experience and is the repository of her passion, however she chooses to express it. It describes her connection to the Divine, regardless of her age or biological reality. It widens the definition of a woman to something other than her reproductive possibilities.

I have used the term Warrior/Lover to describe this fourth aspect because this terminology is personally meaningful to me. However, the basic idea is that the fourth face is a mystery. It is entirely dependent on the experience of the person who calls upon her. She could easily be called the Anchorite, the Teacher, the Healer, the Judge, or Soror. The act of naming her is an exercise in self-identification and, in my opinion, is one of the most radical acts Neopagans (especially women) can embark upon. It cannot be overemphasized how much power is derived from language. To name the fourth face directly connects one to the evolution of the Goddess. It is a creative act that functions as a conduit for manifestation of a new ideal. This act also connects the reader with the wider literary tradition of esoteric fiction described in this book.

Each of the authors described in this study translated their ideals and personal experiences into images of female power through the interrelated concepts of the priestess and the Goddess. Their ideas have profoundly shaped the direction of Goddess worship in the West in the modern era. Helena P. Blavatsky introduced her concept of female divinity to the West as Isis. Dion Fortune drew on her experience with the Western Mystery Tradition to present her image of the dualistic Black and White Isis. Marion Zimmer Bradley drew on her background of esoteric Christianity and feminist spirituality to present her concept of the Triple Goddess. Diana L. Paxson utilizes her education in historical literature and Neopaganism experience to describe various regional goddesses and personal deities. This book has been an attempt to describe the methods employed by these women to reveal and encourage an evolving concept of the Goddess, and to make these methods accessible to the reader who wishes to move beyond the simple consumption of these ideas and into active participation in the dialogue.

Begin with your own experience. Personality is shaped by the experience of our formative years. Our responses and subsequent actions define the rest of our lives. A key component to participation is to analyze your experience and use it as a starting point to describe your ideal vision of both priestess and Goddess. One does not have to reject the previous versions of these concepts in order to do this; the important point is to explain why these ideas are meaningful to you. If you connect with a historical name, then use that; ancient names have power. But do not be afraid to let your imagination wander, and if a new name comes to you, use it instead.

Another technique employed by the authors described in this book is the use of trance writing in the creation of their fiction. The appendix included after this chapter describes an exercise designed to facilitate this state. The last part in the process is to directly communicate with like-minded people, both in print and in person. This method has been successfully used in the past to introduce and deepen Goddess theology throughout the twentieth century; it will be interesting to see whether those results can be replicated in the future.

The Warrior and the Lover

Each incarnation of the priestess in literature gives us a snapshot of the current events and culture of the time in which she is penned. Whether the setting of her story takes place in the mythological past, technological future, or even an alternate dimension, the priestess is always a political character. Her challenges reflect the experience and social concerns of her creator. She is a presentation of the ideal woman in service of the female Divine. This woman uses her body and soul to connect with the Goddess and to manifest this energy to others. Every woman is a reflection of the Divine, so therefore every woman has the capacity to be a priestess.

Each of the authors in esoteric fiction uses the power of language to redefine this character for her generation and to create dialogue about the social concerns that most interest her. This genre is one of the few in which authors can propose radical solutions to the most disturbing issues of their era because they utilize a symbolic language that enables them to experiment with these concepts.

In addition to being aspects of the Goddess, the images of the Warrior and Lover can also be used to classify the different types of priestesses that serve her. Dion Fortune's characters often embody concepts connected to the Lover; those of Marion Zimmer Bradley are firmly on the side of the Warrior. Diana L.

Paxson often has her characters display traits of both or presents multiple women to fill these roles.

Writing at the beginning of the twentieth century, Dion Fortune's ideal priestess was economically independent, freed from the constraints and obligations of domestic life, highly educated, and sexually unrepressed. The priestess is the Initiator and uses her power to heal the wounded aspects of her partner's psyche.

In the midst of the feminism that characterized the mid-twentieth century, Marion Zimmer Bradley's priestess demonstrates a strong commitment to building a community of women, providing a sanctuary for personal growth that is independent of masculine control, and preserving that integrity and independence. Her character uses her power to protect the traditions and authority of the Goddess worshipers.

Writing at the end of the twentieth century, Diana L. Paxson's ideal priestess is a pragmatist who affirms the importance of personal choice and demonstrates the need for tradition as well as progress. This priestess advocates multiculturalism and uses her power to unite men and women together in the midst of cultural chaos and environmental challenge. Every priestess is the living link between man and the Goddess; whether she be daughter, mother, or sage, the power of the warrior/lover is available for her use at any time. Ultimately the priestess is a healer who uses her power to propel the spiritual development of her culture to new heights.

While the image of the warrior/lover can be empowering, exercising this power includes an element of danger. The intensity of the energy that she manifests does not allow for simple interpretations. In my mind, the two sides of this aspect represent the power inherent in the extreme limits of human passion. She is aroused in moments of great need. She comes in response to (and is fueled by) intense circumstances that are often extremely negative. Her ability to enchant the imagination despite these discordant origins transforms painful experience into a legitimate source of radical female power. The warrior/lover breaks the rules and shines a light on the darkest aspects of our society. She does this through forcing us to acknowledge bitter and shameful truths about the world that we live in; however, this process also grants us the language needed to create positive solutions. In order to understand the full potential of this concept, I was forced to examine how she entered my life.

Like many, my childhood was not ideal. In order to tolerate (or retreat from) the conflict of my life, I developed a voracious appetite for books, particularly those that featured tales of female empowerment. As previously stated, my favorite stories, the go-to books, were always the ones that either featured witches, warriors, priestesses, or sorceresses. A really great pick would feature all of them engaged in battle or working as a team. Oftentimes the female protagonist would combine elements of the different themes, but another presentation is to split the attributes between several characters.

If this last technique is employed, the warrior is often the companion of the priestess/sorceress. Both aspects are related through the concept of emancipation. The warrior represents physical empowerment; the other, mental freedom. Combining ideas of power and discipline, the warrior is the female champion of a gender war that seems to exist throughout space and time. She represents the struggle for autonomy, recognition, and the right to exist peacefully in accordance with one's will. Protector of babies and innocents, she is also the mercenary who is hired to enact revenge or wage war. She embodies a message of fierce hope and the end of oppression. Fueled by fury, her methods are combustible. Violence and death are her tools, and killing is her trade. She ushers in a new reality by burning the old one down.

When I was younger, it did not occur to me to question the sustainability of this ideal. The challenges of establishing an independent identity, moving out on my own, and pursuing an alternative spiritual path provided ample opportunity to utilize the endurance of the warrior. She is inventive, an entrepreneur, and a survivor of many campaigns. However, the warrior is also a product of the ultimate breakdown of societal norms and arrives amidst great chaos and despair. Her story often begins when the men are incapacitated or turned savage, and she must utilize her own resources for self-preservation to become her own hero. She has learned to fight primarily in response to violence and to right wrongs perpetuated against herself and other women. These negative origins are not easily averted. Her aims may be righteous, but her methods are not.

The warrior comes to win the fight, which often involves actions that are morally grey. She thrives off of conflict in order to reach her full potential. Whether she is defender or aggressor, her presence is not arbitrary. She steps out of the void to create radical change. But what happens once the fight is won and peace is restored? Without a worthy cause to expend this energy, the power of the warrior can degenerate into something self-destructive. It is important to find constructive ways to neutralize this power when the battle is over, before it reverts into anger, rage, or despair.

As there are many aspects of contemporary culture that create conditions of psychological wounding, it is easy to fall into this trap. This negative energy can manifest as PTSD, or post-traumatic stress disorder. At the time of this writing, suicide is the number one cause of death for soldiers in the United States. Learning about the families affected by these tragedies and knowing active-duty Pagan soldiers, this information troubles me deeply. I now ask different questions about the nature of the warrior. Does she perpetuate a culture of violence and glorify war? Do the gifts that the warrior grants us in battle come with a spiritual price? How does the concept of the Goddess as a warrior coincide with a message of divine love?

The mirror image of the warrior is that of the lover. In fiction she is typically depicted as the priestess, the symbol of sacred sexuality, or the sorceress, possessor of arcane sexual techniques. In Western esotericism the lover has also been known as the scarlet woman, or sacred harlot/whore. (This is not meant to be a pejorative description but instead is supposed to signify her unmarried and non-virginal status. However, the traditional names are clearly problematical for those who object to the negative connotations of these terms.) She embodies the concept of absolute sexual freedom and is not bound to the observance of societal conventions. She represents the healing and radical power of forbidden love and gives herself to her chosen companions regardless of age, race, gender, or caste. She is the lover of all and refuses none that can pay her price. This fee is not necessarily monetary, but it always involves a sacrifice of some sort. She is fueled by the same passion as the warrior, but instead of blood-lust this power manifests as carnal lust in her hands. She may or may not be aggressive, but she is always persuasive. The lover is the most controversial image of female power that I have yet encountered, primarily because unbridled female sexuality is still perceived as the greatest threat to society by men and women alike.

The warrior and lover represent opposite extremes of a shared ideal. These images are connected, as they depict women utilizing their personal power in professions outside of the traditional family unit. Each serves a nonreproductive function in society and exemplifies woman as the entrepreneur in the sense that she chooses to utilize her personal power as she sees fit. However, she does not always enter this path willingly. Oftentimes, the warrior/lover must utilize nontraditional means to regain a sense of self and personal power that has been taken from her. She represents a type of power that is accessible only to those who have been pushed outside of the boundaries of conventional society by force or by choice. The warrior protects the lover in her quest of expanding the definition of sacred sexuality, and the lover transmutes the pain and cruelty that accompany the warrior into joy and redemption.

There is a commercial element inherent to both aspects as they receive monetary compensation for their services. This last point is distinct because it acts as an exonerating detail for the warrior and a damning one for the lover. During war, it is acceptable for the warrior to receive payment for reprehensible acts, which are considered just part of the job. However, it is considered dishonorable for the lover to accept payment for her time. In fiction, the priestess is able to sidestep this taint if the donation is made to the temple or the forfeit is of a spiritual nature, such as in an initiatory setting. However, the sorceress does not usually get a pass if she accepts the gift or admits to enjoying the pleasure of the sexual act. Even if she does not receive payment, the sorceress is often still cast in a negative light for engaging in sexual experimentation without a procreative focus.

Disconnects such as this in the narrative function as clues. They point to the secret potential hidden within societal taboo. In order to unlock the power of this concept, it is first necessary to acknowledge the negative realities connected to this motif. Just as the ideal of the warrior contains a dark reality, so too does the image of the lover. Despite the concepts of sexual freedom and physical autonomy associated with the ideal of the lover, women who attempt to manifest this concept in their own lives often receive negative cultural stigma and personal attack because they operate outside of the protection of the dominant paradigm. Cultural stigma presents itself as social ostracism—the contemporary equivalent of receiving the scarlet letter. With the interconnectedness of social media, this is not an insignificant problem. A maligned reputation can threaten careers, destroy families, and ruin lives. It may even cause people to commit suicide if they feel publicly shamed beyond redemption.

Physical attack can come in many forms. People who are perceived as outside of the system are easy targets for violence. This can manifest as rape, forced prostitution, and sexual enslavement. Sex trafficking is a booming business, and it is a global pandemic. From the highest levels of society to suburban America, it occurs on a daily basis and is closer than you think.

However, there is a distinct difference between those forced into an oppressive situation and those who choose to engage in the sex trade by choice. Living in Holland, where prostitution is legal, allowed me to converse with several women engaged in the sex trade. Some seemed in control of their situations; others were not. One girl I met from the Balkans was not exactly proud of her profession but was adamant that it was much better than going home. She claimed that nothing that had happened in her new situation could compare to the degradation she was living with before in her isolated mountain village. At least here she had a place of her own and kept company only when she wished. But she did state that it was not like this for everyone. She also claimed to have known girls who were lured to the city with promises of modeling or other professional jobs and then displayed in a window without consent.

I left the conversation feeling conflicted. Some people found themselves trapped in the nightmare of being trafficked, whereas others claimed emancipation through employment in the sex trade. I became aware of a strange relationship that connected these separate stories. It is apparent that both victim and willing participant are placed outside of the normal protections of the dominant paradigm. Regardless of whether they are trafficked or traders, both share the same cultural stigma of being perceived as faceless and dishonored.

When I submitted the application for my overseas residential permit, there was a box to check if I was seeking amnesty as a victim of sex trafficking. The idea really shook me up. So innocuous—just another box on a standard form—here was an open acknowledgment of such an ugly reality. Two pages later was the box to check for a student visa. Two pages was all that distinguished my status in this country as a privileged guest from powerless victim.

At first I was upset, but then I realized that at least they had a box to check and recognized the problem with a systemic procedure in place to help. As distasteful and unsettling as it was, naming the problem gave it visibility and imparted a new awareness of these issues to me. I had a stronger response to that form than I had in my previous research on these topics mainly because by forcing me to identify whether I was a victim or not brought the conversation out of an abstract ideal and into a personal level.

I started thinking about an alternate universe in which I would have checked that box, and the reasons that would drive a person to seek asylum in a different country. Despite the terrible experiences that I imagined for that alternate me, and a completely divergent timeline of life events, I realized that our goals would have been the same: simple freedom; mental and physical emancipation; the right to think, act, and love as we wished, without coercion or regret. The space to just be, without fear, with bodily and spiritual integrity intact.

Naming is an empowering act. It allows us to solve problems and create change in our world. These solutions may not be immediate, but they are at least conceivable. Without a name, the problems remain unapproachable. With a name, you have the language to form a plan. Esoteric fiction has provided a space and a symbolic language for women to discuss the failures of the dominant paradigm and rework images of despair into strength.

For me, naming the Goddess as both Warrior and Lover allows access to the positive benefits associated with these archetypes.

It grants a language that I can use to work through the negative energies and feelings that arise from my own experiences. It can also help others who need a framework in order to describe their own challenges and access their own personal power. Finally, identifying the Warrior/Lover as a priestess gives me the necessary tools to transmute this pain into enlightenment. The language gives a context to controversial ideas that cannot be expressed in any other way. This approach is a type of personal alchemy, and the results are not immediate. A lifetime of lead may only translate into a handful of gold, but that dust is precious nonetheless.

Esoteric fiction provides a forum that has united women throughout the twentieth century to debate the relevant concerns of their times, propose solutions to societal ills, and depict woman as divine. The objective for the twenty-first century has not changed, though the topics will reflect the concerns of the current era. These may include but are not limited to the following: endless war, commercialization of sex and violence, personal privacy vs. public interest, and sexual freedom vs. sexual taboo. This last subject would be especially interesting to explore in regards to how women view themselves in relation to other women, and how this dialogue alters when men are introduced to the discussion.

Future conversation will be directed by new interpretations of the priestess, who heralds the next frontier of social and spiritual evolution. It is my sincere wish that authors in this genre will continue to explore the most controversial challenges of our times in effort to create fantastic visions of the Goddess and the societies that venerate her. The audience, in turn, will be stimulated by these ideas and extrapolate viable solutions, spinning straw into gold. It may sound like science fiction, but this is the process that has been documented in the preceding chapters, and it has been successfully utilized for more than a century.

This is entirely achievable. With courage in our hearts, bound only by the limits of our imaginations, we can transmute the dark to manifest the light.

Appendix

Chapter 1 Review Questions:
Women, Literature, and the Occult....

- What is occultism? Describe one of the main goals of this movement.
- What is the link between esoteric societies and first-wave feminism? Name two political movements that have been influenced by metaphysical and occult philosophy.
- Who is Helena Petrovna Blavatsky?
- Name three influential female science-fiction writers from the modern era.
- What are "cons"?
- Name two contemporary religious movements that have been influenced by science fiction.
- What is the relationship between fears and dreams in the context of cultural studies?
- What is biological determinism?
- Name the four aspects of the "Grand Woman" of the Victorian era described by Nina Auerbach. What unique element makes these depictions so different from the renditions of women in art and literature from previous eras?
- Describe some popular depictions of the female demonic. What do angels and mermaids have in common?

Discussion Questions

- What is the difference between a hero and a heroine? Pick two of your favorite stories, and compare and contrast the characters of each. Are there any patterns that arise?
- Pick three movies that feature concepts of the female demonic as protagonists. How have negative images been translated into positive connotations for the female characters in these films?
- Imagine yourself and three of your closest friends as different aspects of the Grand Woman. Which one did you choose, and why?

Chapter 2 Review Questions: Dion Fortune/Violet Firth

- What event does Dion Fortune credit as being the catalyst for her early interest in occult topics?
- Name three strands of religious or metaphysical philosophy that influenced Dion Fortune's work.
- What international conflict coincided with the end of Fortune's fictional output?
- Name three of Dion Fortune's biographers.
- What is anecdotal bias, and why is it problematical?
- Why is the fictional priestess such an important character in the context of religious studies?
- What is trance writing?
- Why is gendered dialogue so significant for Western esotericism?

- Name the two types of priestess that characterize Dion Fortune's fiction.

Discussion Questions

- What does the character of the priestess represent to you?
- Imagine someone else writing the biography of your life. Which events would they highlight as significant to your accomplishments and personal philosophy?
- Have you ever experimented with hypnosis? Describe your experience. Was it positive, negative, or neutral?

Chapter 3 Review Questions: Earth Mother/Moon Mistress

- How does the priestess interact with her male counterparts in Dion Fortune's novels? How does she help them?
- What are the differences between the characters of Earth Mother and Moon Mistress? How are they similar?
- How do the facets of the Grand Woman connect with Fortune's concept of the modern priestess?
- According to Fortune, what is the essential element that the "modest" woman lacks?
- Give an example of gender role reversal from Fortune's fiction. What is the significance of the narrator being male or female in the story?
- Why is Moon Mistress unmarried?
- How does the theme of reincarnation tie into the mythology of the priestess?

- What is the final "safety valve" that may be employed to prevent a state of mental imbalance in the participants of the ritual outlined in the novels?
- Describe the significance of color in the construction of the Goddess in Fortune's works. What is the relationship between the White and Black Isis?
- What does the veil symbolize?

Discussion Questions

- Find a story you enjoy that is narrated by a character with a gender other than your own. Is the author speaking from their own gender or another? Write a short story in which you narrate the piece from an opposite perspective.
- What are your thoughts on reincarnation? Describe your own theories, then write a short piece rebutting your original position.
- Discover three religions that require female participants to wear veils or head coverings. Describe the significance of this article of clothing in each context.

Chapter 4 Review Questions: Marion Zimmer Bradley

- What is the title of Marion Zimmer Bradley's most famous book?
- During which time frame were the Darkover novels created?
- What is the name of the periodical published by the Daughters of Bilitis in the mid-twentieth century?
- Is Marion Zimmer Bradley a feminist?

- How does alternating between first- and third-person perspective enhance the story of the priestess? Which author devised this original template?
- What are some of the religious and metaphysical philosophies that have influenced the works of MZB?
- What is the SCA?
- What is the name of the anthology edited by MZB in the 1980s that featured stories depicting radical reinterpretations of female power?
- What is the name of the famous residence in Berkeley that served as both a family home and a writing collective?

Discussion Questions

- Why would an author choose to write under an assumed name? What are the benefits and disadvantages of this strategy?
- Describe some of the rapid cultural and political changes that have occurred in the West throughout the twentieth century. Pick a decade from this time and imagine what a day in your life would include. What type of music, literature, and activities would you enjoy?
- Picture yourself involved in an artistic collective. Would you be a resident or a visitor? Describe what your ideal community would resemble. What are some of the challenges that might develop?

Chapter 5 Review Questions: Witch Queen

- Describe the Witch Queen. How is she different from her predecessors?
- Which story contains the bulk of MZB's Atlantean theories?
- How does the theme of reincarnation connect the various characters in Bradley's books?
- What is an anti-hero? Give an example of this type of character from *The Mists of Avalon*.
- What is the "Great Marriage"?
- In esoteric fiction, what is the source of female power? What is the source of feminine evil?
- What is the primary difference between the initiatory structure of the priestess described in the fictional works of Dion Fortune and Marion Zimmer Bradley?
- What is the name of the hidden or fourth face of the Goddess in Bradley's fiction?
- What are the similarities between Moon Mistress and Witch Queen? How are they different?

Discussion Questions

- If you were to compose a story of your life, would you be the hero or the anti-hero?
- Do you prefer to work on your own or as part of a group when it comes to creative projects? Give an instance of when you have attempted group projects as opposed to solo works.
- What are your thoughts on the concept of the "Great Marriage"?

Chapter 6 Review Questions:
Diana L. Paxson

- How is Diana L. Paxson connected to Marion Zimmer Bradley?
- Name some of the religious and metaphysical influences that inspire Paxson's work.
- Describe some of the political and cultural issues that Paxson credits as influences.
- What is the name of the women's group that was created at Greyhaven in the late 1970s?
- Which books of the Avalon series are authored by Diana L. Paxson?
- According to Paxson, which book in the Avalon series is least connected to MZB's concepts?
- How does the concept of fidelity correlate with sexual freedom in Paxson's rendition of the priestess?
- In her own words, how does Paxson distinguish the sorceress from the priestess?
- Name two repeating patterns that Paxson explores in her characters and plot development.
- How does Paxson describe the symbolism of the sword in her novels?

Discussion Questions

- Describe the duties of the Lady of the Land. How would this character function in an urban environment?
- How have your own spiritual or religious ideas changed over the course of your life? Can you recall the images and ideas

that influenced you in the past? Has your focus changed since then?

- What does the image of the sword signify for you?

Chapter 7 Review Questions: Warrior Queen

- Describe the two facets of the Sacred Queen motif explored in the Avalon series.
- What are the unique characteristics of the Warrior Queen? How does she differ from her predecessors?
- Is the Lady of the Land a spiritual or political figure?
- Describe the concept of sovereignty as presented in Paxson's work.
- How are men incorporated into the mythology of the Warrior Queen?
- Cite some of the components of early education in the Avalon series.
- Give an example of the theme of innovation vs. tradition explored by Paxson in the Avalon novels.
- How do Paxson's characters relate to the priestesses presented in Fortune's novels?
- When Boudica has her vision before the final battle in *Ravens of Avalon*, to whom is she speaking?
- How is ancestor worship incorporated into the Avalon mythos?

Discussion Questions

- Do you favor a transcendental or personal interpretation of deity? Why?

- Would you appreciate a theocracy if it was female oriented? What is your take on the blending of religion and politics as expressed in the Avalon series?
- What is your reaction to the concept of the Sacrificial Queen? Is this an image that resonates with you or is it one that you reject?

Chapter 8 Review Questions:
The Priestess and the Problem of Feminine Evil

- Who is the woman with the severed head in popular Victorian iconography?
- What is the difference between celebrating cultural identity and racism?
- What are the two paths of spiritual enlightenment described in the works of Helena P. Blavatsky? Explain the concept of renunciation and how it is explicated by subsequent authors.
- What is the difference between a group soul and a group mind?
- Describe the Law of Polarity and its importance in Western esotericism.
- How does sexual dimorphism determine the role of the priestess?
- Define eugenics. Why is this topic relevant to esoteric discourse in general and the concept of the priestess in particular?
- Why does social taboo often originate from sexual taboo?
- How is feminine evil portrayed in the works reviewed in this study? How does it change from one author to another, and what are the elements that remain constant?

- Who are the saji?
- How does the priestess view abortion? How do the different authors handle this topic?

Discussion Questions

- What are your thoughts on the concept of feminine evil? Are they consistent with the images portrayed in these novels or are they divergent?
- Describe your thoughts or personal philosophy about sacred sexuality. What is permitted and what is taboo?
- Is it racist to celebrate cultural identity? How have these issues influenced your own experience?
- What is your opinion of contraception and abortion? If you could create a perfect society, how would these issues be addressed?

Chapter 9 Review Questions: New Frontiers

- What is an ordeal?
- Describe the greatest gift that humans share. How does it manifest?
- What is the antidote to mental laziness?
- Why is it important to preserve the study of humanities and related currents?
- What are the benefits of venerating the reproductive and aging processes? Describe some of the limitations with this approach.
- How many phases does the moon have?
- Why is personal experience important?

- Who is the Warrior? How is she related to the Lover? Which figure is the most controversial?
- Describe the shared commercial aspect of the Warrior and the Lover. What is the disconnect between the two?
- Why is naming an empowering act?

Discussion Questions

- What would the fourth face of the Goddess look like for you? What is her name?
- Describe a time in your life which challenged or changed your personal philosophy. What methods or ideas have traveled with you from that time, and which ones have you discarded?
- If you could explore any topic or learn any subject, what would you pursue?
- Imagine your perfect society set in the future. Which ideals are held sacred and which ones are feared?

Exercise

AUTOMATIC WRITING

THE PURPOSE OF this exercise is to explore the process of trance or automatic writing in an effort to connect with the Goddess. While this method is reminiscent of the techniques utilized by female authors, the process is open to anyone and can be useful for men and women who wish to explore or deepen their understanding of the anima, or internal representation of the female ideal; in previous experiments, male and female participants have reported success with utilizing the following technique.

If you are experimenting alone, it may be useful to record the meditation or invocation in advance so that your mind may relax while you write. If you are experimenting with a friend or amongst a group, you may wish to designate someone to facilitate the experience by narrating the invocation in the exercise or similar poetry or prose that serves to focus the group toward connection with the Goddess. One example could be a recitation of the Charge of the Goddess or something similar that appeals to you. Although this exercise is written with the solo practitioner in mind, it is designed with the intention for you to share your results with others. Creating sacred space is essential to produce results. Be mindful of the energies that you wish to align with, and set up an altar that incorporates symbolism that achieves this goal. Scents, sounds, and colors are all tools that may be used to enhance the experience.

You will need the following items:

- candle
- deck of tarot or playing cards
- small hand mirror
- several sheets of paper
- pen

Find a private space in which to work, with a table or writing desk on which to place your assembled supplies. Place your mirror in the center of the table, positioned so that you can glimpse your eyes in its surface from your chair. Remove the four queens from your deck of cards and arrange them in a circle around the mirror, with the Queen of Pentacles or Diamonds above the center, followed by the Queen of Swords or Spades to the right, Queen of Wands or Clubs below, and finally the Queen of Cups or Hearts placed to the left of the mirror.

The symbol you have created is known as the quincunx. This ancient glyph has been used throughout history, and its most simple depiction is four dots arranged around a fifth point. One interpretation of this arrangement can be understood as the representation of the energies of the four terrestrial elements of earth, air, fire, and water, with the quintessence, or fifth element—referred to as aether in classical antiquity and alchemical texts—in the center. This fifth element was considered to be of a celestial nature, a mysterious substance that made up the heavens yet was rumored to be present in minute amounts in the material realm as the connection between the terrestrial and the Divine.

For the purposes of this exercise, the cards represent the four faces of the Goddess, their energies converging on a center point, symbolized by the mirror. Place your pen in your dominant hand, resting it atop the paper, ready to go. Make yourself comfortable. When you are satisfied with the arrangement of your altar, light the candle and close your eyes. Begin with a measured breathing, slow and steady, using this time to calm and clear your mind. Take a few minutes to relax.

When you are ready, employ the technique of the fourfold breath. Count or tap a steady rhythm of four beats as you breathe in for four beats, hold for four beats, slowly exhale for four beats, and empty hold for four beats. Continue this method as long as feels comfortable for you, keeping your eyes closed. When ready, begin slowly moving your writing instrument lightly over your paper and recite the following words:

Day and night, dawn and dusk
Love and light, death and lust
Lady of the four-spoked wheel
Revealed within the ancient seal

Open your eyes and look into the mirror in the center of the table. Allow your vision to become unfocused; open your awareness to the experience. Begin writing immediately, capturing any images or impressions that come to you. Do not be concerned with form or content, just write whatever comes to you in stream of consciousness. Keep writing, keeping up the pace until you are satisfied or until nothing else can be recorded. This part can become quite frantic, sometimes chaotic; allow pages to fall to the ground if necessary to keep your pen constantly in motion. Words, doodles, whatever comes out—just keep your hand moving until you run out of steam. When done, place your pen on the table. Take a deep breath in and then let everything out in a final cathartic exhalation.

When you are ready, review what you have created. Are there words or images that inspire you to further explication? Has some type of drawing or sigil developed on the page? Do not be concerned if your entry appears to be entirely nonsensical, just record your results in your typical manner. In a few days, or when you are able, repeat the experiment and record your results. This method is designed to develop the talent of automatic writing, so remember to be open to the experience and not worry about striving for perfection. Practice will facilitate the flow. The point is to record whatever impressions or messages come to you, and then review them later for translation. Sometimes only snippets can be deciphered, but you may be surprised by the complexity of certain ideas that arise. Be sure to share your results with a friend or, better yet, invite your companion to participate and then compare notes.

The purpose of this exercise is not only to strengthen one's ability to connect with the fourfold Goddess but also to foster a dialogue that explores these ideas within a larger community.

ACKNOWLEDGMENTS

A PROJECT OF this magnitude is not accomplished in a vacuum. There are numerous people for me to thank, but there are a few folks who deserve a special acknowledgment.

First and foremost, I need to thank my lovely husband, Marc, who has weathered this entire endeavor, for his encouragement, love, and continued support. Without him, none of this would have materialized.

A huge thanks to my wonderful friends at Serpent's Song, a.k.a Research and Development, for their patience and participation in my ongoing thought experiments. I am humbled and honored to be working with such a fantastic group.

Much gratitude to my friends at Divine Guidance, who have offered enthusiasm and positive energy to the final stretch of this project.

And finally, I wish to acknowledge the numerous teachers and friends who have influenced and encouraged me throughout this journey. While everyone may be familiar with the adage "when the student is ready, the teacher appears," I have had the good fortune to claim many teachers and companions along the way. Special thanks to all of the seekers, guides, magicians, artists, dreamers, deviants, and solid citizens who have shared their wisdom and experience with me. Blessings and much love to you all!

Permission to quote from the sources in this book is gratefully acknowledged from the following:

> Material excerpted from the following Dion Fortune titles: *The Goat Foot God, The Sea Priestess, Moon Magic, Ceremonial Magic Unveiled* (Occult Review), *The Cosmic Doctrine, Psychic Self-Defense,* and *The Secrets of Dr. Tavernier* © Society of Inner Light with permission from Red Wheel/Weiser, LLC, Newburyport, MA, and San Francisco, CA; www.redwheelweiser.com.

> Material excerpted from the following Marion Zimmer Bradley titles: *The Mists of Avalon, The Firebrand, The Fall of Atlantis, Greyhaven, Sword and Sorceress Vol. I,* and *Thendara House* reprinted by permission of the Marion Zimmer Bradley Literary Works Trust and Scovil Galen Ghosh Literary Agency, Inc.

> Material excerpted from Diana L. Paxson is reprinted by permission of the author and the author's agents, Scovil Galen Ghosh Literary Agency, Inc.

> Material excerpted from Nina Auerbach's *Woman and the Demon* (pp. 2, 63, 83, 107, 114, 162, and 180) is reprinted by permission of the publisher, Harvard University Press, Cambridge, Mass., © 1982 by the President and Fellows of Harvard College.

> Material excerpted from Joy Dixon's *Divine Feminine: Theosophy and Feminism in England* (pp. 6, 205, 214) is reprinted with permission of The Johns Hopkins University Press © 2001.

> Material excerpted from Ronald Hutton's *Triumph of the Moon: A History of Modern Pagan Witchcraft* (2001) is reprinted by permission of Oxford University Press.

BIBLIOGRAPHY

Arbur, Rosemarie. *Leigh Brackett, Marion Zimmer Bradley, Anne McCaffrey: A Primary and Secondary Bibliography.* Boston: G. K. Hall & Co., 1982.

———. *Marion Zimmer Bradley, Starmont Reader's Guide 27.* Mercer Island, WA: Starmont House, Inc., 1985.

Auerbach, Nina. *Woman and the Demon: The Life of a Victorian Myth.* Cambridge: Harvard University Press, 1982.

Bradley, Marion Zimmer. *The Fall of Atlantis.* New York: Baen Publishing Enterprises, 1983.

———. *The Firebrand.* New York: Simon & Schuster, Inc., 1987.

———. *The Mists of Avalon.* New York: Ballantine Books, 1982.

———. *Sword and Sorceress.* New York: DAW Books, 1984.

Chapman, Janine. *Quest for Dion Fortune.* York Beach, ME: Samuel Weiser, Inc., 1993.

Dijkstra, Bram. *Evil Sisters.* New York: Alfred A. Knopf, 1996.

———. *Idols of Perversity.* New York: Oxford University Press, 1986.

Dixon, Joy. *Divine Feminine: Theosophy and Feminism in England*. Baltimore, MD: The Johns Hopkins University Press, 2001.

Fanger, Claire. *Dictionary of Gnosis and Western Esotericism*, s.v. "Fortune, Dion" in Hanegraaf, et al., *Dictionary of Gnosis and Western Esotericism*, vol. 1. Leiden: Brill Academic Publishers, 2005.

Fielding, Charles, and Carr Collins. *The Story of Dion Fortune*. Dallas, TX: Star & Cross, 1985.

Fortune, Dion. "Ceremonial Magic Unveiled" in *The Occult Review* (Jan. 1933), 13–24.

———. *The Cosmic Doctrine*. London: The Society of Inner Light, 1949.

———. *The Goat Foot God*. London: The Aquarian Press, 1936.

———. *Moon Magic: Being the Memoirs of a Mistress of That Art*. London: The Aquarian Press, 1956.

———. *The Mystical Qabalah*. Boston: Red Wheel/Weiser, 2000.

———. *Psychic Self-Defense*. Boston: Red Wheel/Weiser, 1930, 1997.

———. *The Sea Priestess*. London: The Inner Light Publishing Co., 1935; Boston: Red Wheel/Weiser, 2003.

———. *The Secrets of Dr. Taverner*. Columbus: Ariel Press, 1992.

Frazer, James G. *The Golden Bough*. New York: Random House, 1890, 1981.

Fuog, Karen E. C. "Imprisoned in the Phallic Oak: Marion Zimmer Bradley and Merlin's Seductress" in *Quondam et Futurus: A Journal of Arthurian Interpretations* 1.1 (spring 1991), 73–88.

Gilbert, Sandra M., and Susan Gubar. *The Madwoman in the Attic*. London: Yale University Press, 1979.

Greer, Mary K. *Women of the Golden Dawn: Rebels and Priestesses*. Rochester, VT: Park Street Press, 1995.

Hanegraaff, Wouter J., in collaboration with Antoine Faivre, Roelof van den Broek, Jean-Pierre Brach, eds. *Dictionary of Gnosis and Western Esotericism*, vol. 1. Leiden: Brill Academic Publishers, 2005.

Hildebrand, Kristina. *The Female Reader at the Round Table: Religion and Women in Three Contemporary Arthurian Texts*. Uppsala: University of Uppsala Press, 2001.

Hutton, Ronald. *The Triumph of the Moon: A History of Modern Pagan Witchcraft*. New York: Oxford University Press, 1999.

Moore, C. L. *Jirel of Joiry*. New York: Ace Books, 1977, 1982.

"MZB's Biography." Marion Zimmer Bradley Literary Works Trust, http://mzbworks.home.att.net/bio.htm.

Noble, James. "*The Mists of Avalon*: A Confused Assault on Patriarchy" in *The Middle Ages after the Middle Ages in the English-speaking World*, ed. Marie-Francoise Alamichel and Derek Brewer, 149–152. Cambridge: Boydell & Brewer Ltd., 1997.

Paxson, Diana L. "Marion Zimmer Bradley and *The Mists of Avalon*" in *Arthuriana* 9.1 (spring 1999), 110–126.

———. *Marion Zimmer Bradley's Ancestors of Avalon*. London: Viking Penguin, 2004.

———. *Marion Zimmer Bradley's The Ravens of Avalon*. London: Viking Penguin, 2007.

———. *Marion Zimmer Bradley's Sword of Avalon*. London: Viking Penguin, 2009.

Richardson, Alan. *Priestess: The Life and Magic of Dion Fortune*. London: Aquarian Press, 1987.

INDEX

Abortion, 72, 134, 136, 144, 150, 151, 186

Anderle, 99–101, 103, 104, 107, 115–120

Angel, 25–28, 44, 49, 52, 81, 138

Antifeminist, 18, 26, 124

Aquarian Order of the Restoration, 63, 86

Archetypes, xiii, xxviii, 8, 9, 38, 52, 66, 73, 74, 79, 80, 100, 103, 173

Arthurian, 60, 62, 66, 71, 90, 96, 103, 115, 197

Ásatrú, 87

Atlantis, 49, 50, 62, 69, 70, 73, 90, 99, 100, 109–111, 135, 137, 141, 143, 144, 146, 194, 195

Automatic writing, xxxii, 40, 189, 192

Avalon, xxii, xxxi, 2, 3, 50, 59–63, 65, 66, 69, 70, 73, 74, 76–78, 82, 83, 87–91, 98–102, 105–113, 115–121, 135–137, 142, 144–147, 149, 150, 182–185, 194, 195, 197, 198

Beltane, 76, 142, 147

Berkeley, 59, 63, 64, 85, 93, 94, 181

Binary gender, 124

Biological determinism, 8, 23, 123–125, 130, 177

Black, 2, 51–54, 70, 81, 82, 100, 145, 164, 180

Black Isis, 2, 51, 53, 54, 70, 100, 180

Blasphemous, 76, 143, 144

Blavatsky, Helena Petrovna, 2, 16, 17, 40, 52, 74, 125–130, 163, 177, 185

Boudica, 107, 111–115, 120, 137, 147, 148, 184

Bradley, Marion Zimmer, xxvi, xxxi, 2, 3, 50, 57–67, 69–83, 85–88, 93, 98, 99, 101, 105, 108, 110, 111, 116, 118, 120, 121, 130, 132, 133, 135–137, 141–147, 150, 152, 164–166, 180, 182, 183, 194, 195, 197, 198

Breen, Walter, 59, 63

Catholicism, 58, 78

Celibacy, 28, 75, 149

Chick lit, xxix

Cons, 21, 94, 177

Contraception, 134, 150, 186

Coven, 80

Covenant of the Goddess, 87

Crone, 2, 4, 81, 88, 103, 159–161, 163

Dark Mother, 3, 4, 9, 70, 73, 81, 99, 100, 120, 136

Darkmoon Circle, 62, 63, 86, 89

Darkover, 58, 59, 89, 130, 135, 180

Darwin, Charles, 22, 23

DeCles, Jon, 85, 92

Degenerative, 27

Demon, xxiv, xxx, 6, 18, 21, 22, 24–29, 38, 42, 44, 45, 49, 52, 72, 81, 82, 104, 113, 115, 138, 144, 166, 177, 178, 194, 195

Deoris, 70, 137, 143, 144

Divine, xxii, xxv, 1, 3, 6, 8, 15, 16, 18, 19, 38, 40–42, 46, 48, 50, 51, 80, 81, 103, 111, 114, 121, 122, 130, 133, 136–138, 144, 145, 159, 162, 163, 165, 169, 174, 191, 193, 194, 196

Domaris, 70, 143

Druidry, 14, 111, 114

Earth Mother, 40–42, 45, 46, 48–50, 55, 73, 75, 81, 105, 107–109, 135, 145, 179

Eastern mysticism and philosophy, 16

Environmentalism, 121

Ethics, 45, 146, 151

Eugenics, 23, 123, 132, 134, 135, 185

Evans, Penry, 34–36

Evil, xiii, xiv, xvi, xxi, xxii, xxxi, 1, 6, 27, 42, 60, 72, 77, 78, 82, 97, 122–124, 138, 139, 141–143, 145, 148–150, 182, 185, 186, 195

Evolution, xxxii, 4, 15, 16, 22, 23, 74, 97, 116, 126–130, 133, 135, 158, 163, 174

Evolutionary psychology, 23

Excalibur, 108, 115, 119, 137

Experiment, xxxii, 38, 40, 44, 165, 192

Fandom, 21, 59

Fecundity, 48, 54, 75, 159, 162

Fellowship of the Spiral Path, 87

Felt, George Henry, xxii, xxvii, 16, 90, 134, 158, 160, 162

Feminism, 1, 5, 6, 15, 18, 20, 26, 59, 72, 90, 127, 134, 166, 177, 194, 196

Fertilization, 132

Fidelity, 95, 96, 148, 183

Firth, Violet, 31, 32, 178

Fortune, Dion, xiv, xxvi, xxxi, 2, 31–33, 36, 40, 41, 52, 60, 62, 71, 78, 86, 88, 90, 95, 96, 98, 99, 102, 120, 124, 130, 131, 138, 164–166, 178, 179, 182, 194–196, 198

Fourfold Goddess, 82, 192

Fraternity of the Inner Light, 33

Freethinking, 15

Gender, xxvi, xxx, 6, 7, 9, 18, 20, 23, 25, 34, 38, 46, 60, 64, 69, 124, 143, 160, 167, 169, 179, 180

Gnosis, 12, 13, 33, 136, 196, 197

Goddess, xix, xxii, xxiii, xxvi, xxviii, xxxii, 1–9, 21, 34, 37, 39, 40, 48, 51–55, 60–63, 69–71, 74–76, 79–83, 87, 91, 95, 97, 99, 100, 102–104, 106, 110, 111, 113–115, 117, 119–123, 136, 137, 143, 145, 148, 150–153, 157–166, 169, 173, 174, 180, 182, 187, 189, 191, 192

Grand Woman, 24, 25, 28, 29, 177–179

Gray Temple, 143, 146

Great Marriage, 74, 107, 108, 144, 182

Great Mother, 70, 71, 110

Greyhaven, 64, 65, 86, 87, 91–94, 183, 194

Group Mind, 130–132, 185

Group Soul, 130, 131, 185

Hearthkeeper, 130

Heathenism, 3, 13, 87

Hermetic Order of the Golden Dawn, 13, 17, 33

Hermeticism, 127

Hrafnar Kindred, 87

Iconography, 8, 24, 25, 51, 52, 185

Initiate, 95, 130

Isis—see White Isis, Black Isis

Jirel of Joiry, 20, 197

Kassandra, 73, 144

King-making, 79, 112

King, Sacrificial, 74, 113, 137

Kingsford, Anna, xxvi, 17

Lackey, Mercedes, 65, 158

Lady, xxvi, 61, 74, 86, 90, 100–103, 106, 113, 115, 116, 118–120, 130, 148, 183, 184, 191

Lady of the Land, 90, 100, 101, 106, 113, 119, 130, 148, 183, 184

Law of Polarity, 132, 185

Le Guin, Ursula K., xiv, xv, 19

Lhiannon, 111, 112, 114, 115, 147, 150, 151

Lilith le Fay, 38–39, 49, 140

Lineage, 3, 73, 79

Literature, xii, xxii, xxiv, xxx, xxxi, 1, 11, 15, 19, 24, 25, 54, 59, 85, 89, 101, 123, 124, 164, 165, 177, 181

Magic, xv, xxi, xxii, xxiv, xxix, xxx, 12, 13, 15, 16, 21, 33, 34, 36–39, 41, 42, 51, 61, 70, 75, 79, 80, 88, 95–99, 102, 107, 110, 112, 123, 125, 127, 133, 136, 139–143, 146, 147, 194, 196, 198

Maiden, 2, 4, 25, 80–82, 88, 103, 110, 159–163

Maitland, Edward, 17

Marriage, 34, 35, 46, 48, 50, 55, 74, 96, 107–109, 112, 125, 130, 132, 139, 142, 144, 148, 182

Mathers, Moina, 33, 59

Mathers, S. L MacGregor, 33

Matriarchal, 60, 62, 71, 76

Mermaid, 26

Micail, 107, 109, 110

Midwife, 108, 150

Mikantor, 104, 107, 115–119, 121

Miscarriage, 144

Miscegenation, 126

Modern, xvi, xx, xxiv, xxx, xxxii, 1, 6, 7, 11, 12, 22, 26, 34, 37, 39, 44, 46–48, 51, 58, 60, 66, 71, 72, 75, 123–125, 129, 138, 141, 157, 162, 163, 177, 179, 194, 197

Modesty, 54, 161

Monogamy, 76, 95, 96

Moon Mistress, 40–42, 48–50, 55, 73, 74, 81, 83, 105, 107, 133, 135, 136, 145, 179, 182

Moore, C. L., 20, 197

Morgaine, 60, 71, 80–82, 100, 136, 137, 142, 144

Morgan le Fay, 38, 49, 60, 70

Morguase, 142

Mother, xiv, 2–4, 8, 9, 23, 25, 40–42, 45, 46, 48–50, 55, 59, 70, 71, 73, 75, 78, 81, 82, 88, 90, 93, 95, 99–101, 103, 105–110, 115–118, 120, 121, 133–136, 138, 139, 143, 145, 159, 161, 163, 166, 179

Motherhood, 78, 80, 125, 130, 134, 135, 144

Nazi, 128

Neopaganism, 5, 8, 13, 21, 37, 65, 164

New Age, 13

New Thought, 13

New Woman, 26, 27, 29

Nonfiction, xv, xviii, 1, 5, 36, 37, 55, 87, 99, 106, 130, 133, 150

Occult, xv, xxii, xxiii, xxvi, xxix, xxxi, 1, 2, 5, 11–14,
    16–18, 21, 31, 33, 36, 46, 48, 55, 60, 77, 95, 124,
    127–131, 142–144, 150, 177, 178, 194, 196

Occultism, xiv, xvi, 13, 15, 31, 41, 43,
    51, 58, 123, 134, 143, 177

Olcott, Henry Steel, 16

Open Way, 129

Paganism, xvii, xx, 13, 34, 44, 49, 86, 87, 90, 158

Pan, 42, 44

Patriarchy, 7, 197

Paxson, Diana L., xxvi, xxxi, xxxii, 3, 62–65, 70, 83, 85–87,
    105, 108, 110–112, 116, 118–122, 130, 132, 133, 135–137,
    145, 146, 148–152, 164, 166, 183, 184, 194, 198

Philosophia perennis, 13, 69

Politics, xxv, xxx, 19, 22, 23, 55, 66, 112, 156, 185

Priestess, xv, xvii, xx, xxii, xxiii, xxvi, xxvii, xxx, xxxii,
    1–3, 5–8, 11, 15, 21, 24, 29, 34, 35, 37–42, 45–51, 54,
    55, 58, 60–63, 66, 67, 69–76, 78–83, 86–92, 95–103,
    105, 106, 110–112, 115–119, 121–124, 130, 132, 133,
    136–146, 148–153, 157, 159, 162–167, 169, 170,
    174, 178, 179, 181–183, 185, 186, 194, 196, 198

Procreation, 51

Promiscuity, 77, 139, 147, 148

Prostitution, 24, 77, 171, 172

Psychic, 31, 46, 74, 109, 135, 143, 194, 196

Queen, xxi, 4, 24, 67, 69, 71, 73–76, 78, 81–83, 95, 96,
    100, 101, 105–109, 111–118, 120–122, 133, 135–137,
    142, 145, 147, 149, 150, 182, 184, 185, 190

INDEX

Quest, xxii, 20, 72, 118, 170, 195

Race, 20, 25, 48, 49, 64, 74, 128, 130–134, 136, 144, 169

Readers, xvi, 7, 15, 21, 36, 38

Religion, xvii, xxi, xxii, xxv, xxvi, xxx, 5, 6, 14, 16, 44, 49, 58, 60, 62, 63, 66, 69–72, 76, 79, 80, 83, 90, 109, 110, 120, 121, 125, 127, 131, 137, 142, 155, 185, 197

Renunciation, 52, 54, 130, 185

Rituals, xxiv, 12, 16, 31, 34, 37, 41, 43, 47, 48, 50, 60, 62, 63, 74–76, 78–80, 87, 88, 91, 92, 97, 107, 108, 111, 112, 115–119, 131, 141, 143, 180

Riveda, 143

Sacred, xxiii, 1, 3, 12, 16, 18, 35, 37, 46, 54, 71, 75, 77, 78, 83, 88, 105–108, 115, 116, 134–137, 142, 144, 145, 147, 150, 152, 169, 170, 184, 186, 187, 190

Saji, 143, 146, 147, 186

Salome, 123, 124, 136

Science, xxi, xxv, 2, 13, 14, 16, 19–22, 64, 124, 125, 127, 128, 133, 175, 177

Science-fiction, xxi, 13, 19–21, 57, 59, 64, 65, 94, 175, 177

Scientology, 21

Seductress, 24, 197

Sex, xxiv, xxxi, 3, 4, 6, 9, 22, 27, 28, 37, 38, 42, 46, 48, 50, 51, 55, 61, 75–77, 95, 96, 107, 108, 117, 119, 124, 133, 142, 145–148, 161, 162, 171, 172, 174

Sexual dimorphism, repression, 24, 44

Shelley, Mary, 19

Siren, 26, 27

Society for Creative Anachronism (SCA), 65, 85, 93, 94, 181

Sorceress, xxxi, 6, 60, 63, 64, 87, 97, 99, 100, 142, 143, 145, 151, 167, 169, 171, 183, 194, 195

Sovereignty, 106, 137, 184

Speculative Fiction, xxxi, 11, 19–21, 58

Spinster, 28, 49, 138

Sword, 4, 6, 8, 63, 64, 87, 91, 99, 100, 102–105, 107, 108, 110, 115, 116, 118–120, 136, 137, 145, 149, 183, 184, 194, 195, 198

Taboo, 8, 10, 45, 77, 122, 126, 140, 141, 159, 171, 174, 185, 186

Tarot, 12, 190, 207

The Troth, 87

Theosophical Society, 13, 14, 16–18, 63, 78, 127, 128

Theosophy, 12, 14, 18, 33, 194, 196

Tiriki, 107, 109–111, 120

Tirilan, 100, 101, 103, 107, 115–120, 149

Traditional, xi, 4, 6, 15, 20, 23–26, 48, 51, 52, 79, 82, 106, 112, 130, 138, 142, 169, 170

Trance writing, xxxii, 2, 15, 39, 164, 178

Tribe, 6, 73, 106–109, 111, 117, 120, 121, 126, 132, 133, 135, 136, 151, 161

Triple Goddess, 2, 9, 80, 82, 103, 120, 122, 157–159, 161–164

Vampire, 27

Velantos, 102, 104, 107, 117, 119

Victorian (morals, concepts), 1, 20, 22–28, 39, 52, 123

Villains, 139, 145

Virginity, 52, 54, 74, 112, 149

Viviane, 80, 99, 101, 144

War, xxiv, 9, 22, 36, 95, 106, 117, 119, 136, 146, 149, 167–170, 174

Warrior, xxi, 4, 8, 9, 72, 81, 83, 105–109, 111–113, 115, 116, 118, 121, 122, 133, 135, 136, 145, 149, 150, 163, 165–171, 173, 174, 184, 187

Western Esotericism, xxv, xxvi, xxx, xxxi, 2, 12–14, 33, 37, 55, 60, 77, 125, 132, 169, 178, 185, 196, 197

White Isis, 53, 82, 145, 164

Whore, 6, 28, 49, 138, 169

Wicca, xvii, xx, xxiii, 14, 89, 96, 158

Witch, xiv, 6, 67, 69, 71, 73–76, 78, 81–83, 105, 107–109, 133, 135, 136, 142, 145, 182

Witchcraft, xvii, xix, xx, 13, 28, 65, 66, 194, 197

Woman, xiv, xxi, xxv, xxvi, xxx, 1, 6, 8, 9, 20, 23–29, 31, 34, 36–39, 44, 45, 48, 51, 53, 55, 57, 60, 66, 72, 76, 79–81, 88, 114, 126, 134, 136, 138, 140–142, 145, 148, 151, 158, 159, 162, 163, 165, 169, 170, 174, 177–179, 185, 194, 195

Woman's Suffrage Movement, 18, 26